Oroonoko a tragedy as it is acted at the Theatre-Royal, by His Majesty's servants / written by Tho. Southerne. (1699)

Thomas Southerne

Oroonoko a tragedy as it is acted at the Theatre-Royal, by His Majesty's servants / written by Tho. Southerne.
Southerne, Thomas, 1660-1746.
[Edition statement:] The second edition.
[5], 58 p.
London : Printed for H. Playford and B. Tooke,
Wing / S4763
English
Reproduction of the original in the Cambridge University Library

Early English Books Online (EEBO) Editions

Imagine holding history in your hands.

Now you can. Digitally preserved and previously accessible only through libraries as Early English Books Online, this rare material is now available in single print editions. Thousands of books written between 1475 and 1700 and ranging from religion to astronomy, medicine to music, can be delivered to your doorstep in individual volumes of high-quality historical reproductions.

We have been compiling these historic treasures for more than 70 years. Long before such a thing as "digital" even existed, ProQuest founder Eugene Power began the noble task of preserving the British Museum's collection on microfilm. He then sought out other rare and endangered titles, providing unparalleled access to these works and collaborating with the world's top academic institutions to make them widely available for the first time. This project furthers that original vision.

These texts have now made the full journey -- from their original printing-press versions available only in rare-book rooms to online library access to new single volumes made possible by the partnership between artifact preservation and modern printing technology. A portion of the proceeds from every book sold supports the libraries and institutions that made this collection possible, and that still work to preserve these invaluable treasures passed down through time.

This is history, traveling through time since the dawn of printing to your own personal library.

Initial Proquest EEBO Print Editions collections include:

Early Literature

This comprehensive collection begins with the famous Elizabethan Era that saw such literary giants as Chaucer, Shakespeare and Marlowe, as well as the introduction of the sonnet. Traveling through Jacobean and Restoration literature, the highlight of this series is the Pollard and Redgrave 1475-1640 selection of the rarest works from the English Renaissance.

Early Documents of World History

This collection combines early English perspectives on world history with documentation of Parliament records, royal decrees and military documents that reveal the delicate balance of Church and State in early English government. For social historians, almanacs and calendars offer insight into daily life of common citizens. This exhaustively complete series presents a thorough picture of history through the English Civil War.

Historical Almanacs

Historically, almanacs served a variety of purposes from the more practical, such as planting and harvesting crops and plotting nautical routes, to predicting the future through the movements of the stars. This collection provides a wide range of consecutive years of "almanacks" and calendars that depict a vast array of everyday life as it was several hundred years ago.

Early History of Astronomy & Space

Humankind has studied the skies for centuries, seeking to find our place in the universe. Some of the most important discoveries in the field of astronomy were made in these texts recorded by ancient stargazers, but almost as impactful were the perspectives of those who considered their discoveries to be heresy. Any independent astronomer will find this an invaluable collection of titles arguing the truth of the cosmic system.

Early History of Industry & Science

Acting as a kind of historical Wall Street, this collection of industry manuals and records explores the thriving industries of construction; textile, especially wool and linen; salt; livestock; and many more.

Early English Wit, Poetry & Satire

The power of literary device was never more in its prime than during this period of history, where a wide array of political and religious satire mocked the status quo and poetry called humankind to transcend the rigors of daily life through love, God or principle. This series comments on historical patterns of the human condition that are still visible today.

Early English Drama & Theatre

This collection needs no introduction, combining the works of some of the greatest canonical writers of all time, including many plays composed for royalty such as Queen Elizabeth I and King Edward VI. In addition, this series includes history and criticism of drama, as well as examinations of technique.

Early History of Travel & Geography

Offering a fascinating view into the perception of the world during the sixteenth and seventeenth centuries, this collection includes accounts of Columbus's discovery of the Americas and encompasses most of the Age of Discovery, during which Europeans and their descendants intensively explored and mapped the world. This series is a wealth of information from some the most groundbreaking explorers.

Early Fables & Fairy Tales

This series includes many translations, some illustrated, of some of the most well-known mythologies of today, including Aesop's Fables and English fairy tales, as well as many Greek, Latin and even Oriental parables and criticism and interpretation on the subject.

Early Documents of Language & Linguistics

The evolution of English and foreign languages is documented in these original texts studying and recording early philology from the study of a variety of languages including Greek, Latin and Chinese, as well as multilingual volumes, to current slang and obscure words. Translations from Latin, Hebrew and Aramaic, grammar treatises and even dictionaries and guides to translation make this collection rich in cultures from around the world.

Early History of the Law

With extensive collections of land tenure and business law "forms" in Great Britain, this is a comprehensive resource for all kinds of early English legal precedents from feudal to constitutional law, Jewish and Jesuit law, laws about public finance to food supply and forestry, and even "immoral conditions." An abundance of law dictionaries, philosophy and history and criticism completes this series.

Early History of Kings, Queens and Royalty

This collection includes debates on the divine right of kings, royal statutes and proclamations, and political ballads and songs as related to a number of English kings and queens, with notable concentrations on foreign rulers King Louis IX and King Louis XIV of France, and King Philip II of Spain. Writings on ancient rulers and royal tradition focus on Scottish and Roman kings, Cleopatra and the Biblical kings Nebuchadnezzar and Solomon.

Early History of Love, Marriage & Sex

Human relationships intrigued and baffled thinkers and writers well before the postmodern age of psychology and self-help. Now readers can access the insights and intricacies of Anglo-Saxon interactions in sex and love, marriage and politics, and the truth that lies somewhere in between action and thought.

Early History of Medicine, Health & Disease

This series includes fascinating studies on the human brain from as early as the 16th century, as well as early studies on the physiological effects of tobacco use. Anatomy texts, medical treatises and wound treatment are also discussed, revealing the exponential development of medical theory and practice over more than two hundred years.

Early History of Logic, Science and Math

The "hard sciences" developed exponentially during the 16th and 17th centuries, both relying upon centuries of tradition and adding to the foundation of modern application, as is evidenced by this extensive collection. This is a rich collection of practical mathematics as applied to business, carpentry and geography as well as explorations of mathematical instruments and arithmetic; logic and logicians such as Aristotle and Socrates; and a number of scientific disciplines from natural history to physics.

Early History of Military, War and Weaponry

Any professional or amateur student of war will thrill at the untold riches in this collection of war theory and practice in the early Western World. The Age of Discovery and Enlightenment was also a time of great political and religious unrest, revealed in accounts of conflicts such as the Wars of the Roses.

Early History of Food

This collection combines the commercial aspects of food handling, preservation and supply to the more specific aspects of canning and preserving, meat carving, brewing beer and even candy-making with fruits and flowers, with a large resource of cookery and recipe books. Not to be forgotten is a "the great eater of Kent," a study in food habits.

Early History of Religion

From the beginning of recorded history we have looked to the heavens for inspiration and guidance. In these early religious documents, sermons, and pamphlets, we see the spiritual impact on the lives of both royalty and the commoner. We also get insights into a clergy that was growing ever more powerful as a political force. This is one of the world's largest collections of religious works of this type, revealing much about our interpretation of the modern church and spirituality.

Early Social Customs

Social customs, human interaction and leisure are the driving force of any culture. These unique and quirky works give us a glimpse of interesting aspects of day-to-day life as it existed in an earlier time. With books on games, sports, traditions, festivals, and hobbies it is one of the most fascinating collections in the series.

The BiblioLife Network

This project was made possible in part by the BiblioLife Network (BLN), a project aimed at addressing some of the huge challenges facing book preservationists around the world. The BLN includes libraries, library networks, archives, subject matter experts, online communities and library service providers. We believe every book ever published should be available as a high-quality print reproduction; printed on-demand anywhere in the world. This insures the ongoing accessibility of the content and helps generate sustainable revenue for the libraries and organizations that work to preserve these important materials.

The following book is in the "public domain" and represents an authentic reproduction of the text as printed by the original publisher. While we have attempted to accurately maintain the integrity of the original work, there are sometimes problems with the original work or the micro-film from which the books were digitized. This can result in minor errors in reproduction. Possible imperfections include missing and blurred pages, poor pictures, markings and other reproduction issues beyond our control. Because this work is culturally important, we have made it available as part of our commitment to protecting, preserving, and promoting the world's literature.

GUIDE TO FOLD-OUTS MAPS and OVERSIZED IMAGES

The book you are reading was digitized from microfilm captured over the past thirty to forty years. Years after the creation of the original microfilm, the book was converted to digital files and made available in an online database.

In an online database, page images do not need to conform to the size restrictions found in a printed book. When converting these images back into a printed bound book, the page sizes are standardized in ways that maintain the detail of the original. For large images, such as fold-out maps, the original page image is split into two or more pages

Guidelines used to determine how to split the page image follows:

• Some images are split vertically; large images require vertical and horizontal splits.
• For horizontal splits, the content is split left to right.
• For vertical splits, the content is split from top to bottom.
• For both vertical and horizontal splits, the image is processed from top left to bottom right.

16THS BRITISH MADE ENGINE DIVIDED

1 2 3 4 5 6

Oroonoko:

A

TRAGEDY,

As it is Acted at the

Theatre-Royal,

By His Majesty's Servants.

Written by *THO. SOUTHERNE*.

Quo fata trahunt, virtus secura sequetur. Lucan.

Virtus recludens immeritis mori
Cælum, negata tentat iter via.

Hor. Od. 2. lib. 3.

The Second Edition.

LONDON:

Printed for *H. Playford* in the *Temple-Change*: And *B. Tooke* at the *Middle-Temple-Gate* in *Fleetstreet*. MDCXCIX.

Persons Reprefented.

MEN.

		BY
Oroonoko,	Mr. *Verbruggen.*
Aboan,	Mr. *Powell.*
Lieutenant-Governor of *Surinam*	Mr. *Williams.*
Blanford,	Mr. *Harland.*
Stanmore,	Mr. *Horden.*
Jack Stanmore,	Mr. *Mills.*
Capt. Driver.	Mr. *Ben. Johnfon.*
Daniel, *Son to Widow* Lackit,	Mr. *Mich. Lee.*
Hottman,	Mr. *Sympfon.*

Planters, Indians, Negroes, Men, Women, and Children.

WOMEN.

		BY
Imoinda,	Mrs. *Rogers.*
Widow Lackit,	Mrs. *Knight.*
Charlot Welldon *in Man's Cloathes,*	Mrs. *Verbruggen.*
Lucy Welldon, *her Sifter,*	Mrs. *Lucas.*

The SCENE *Surinam,* a Colony in the *Weft-Indies;* at the Time of the Action of this Tragedy, in the Poffeffion of the *English.*

To His GRACE
WILLIAM
Duke of Devonshire, &c.

Lord Steward of His Majesty's Houshold, Knight of the Most Noble Order of the Garter, and One of His Majesty's Most Honourable Privy-Council.

MY LORD,

THE Best part of the Fortune of my last Play (*The Innocent Adultery*) was, that it gave me an Opportunity of making my self known to your Grace. You were pleased to countenance the Advances which I had been a great while directing and aiming at You, and have since encourag'd me into an Industry, which, I hope, will allow me in this Play to own (which is the only way I can) the great Obligation I have to You.

I stand engag'd to Mrs. *Behn* for the Occasion of a most Passionate Distress in my last Play; and in a Conscience that I had not made her a sufficient Acknowledgment, I have run further into her Debt for *Oroonoko*, with a Design to oblige me to be honest; and that every one may find me out for Ingratitude, when I don't say all that's fit for me upon that Subject. She had a great Command of the Stage; and I have often wonder'd that she would bury her Favourite Hero in a *Novel*, when she might have reviv'd him in the *Scene*. She thought either that no Actor could represent him; or she could not bear him represented: And I believe the last, when I remember what I have heard from a Friend of hers, That she always told his Story more feelingly than she writ it. Whatever happen'd to him at *Surinam*, he has mended his Condition in *England*. He was born here under Your Grace's Influence; and that has carried his Fortune farther into the World, than all the Poetical Stars that I could have sollicited for his Success. It

WAS

was Your Opinion, *My Lord*, that directed me to Mr. *Verbruggen*; and it was his Care to maintain Your Opinion, that directed the Town to me, the Better Part of it, the People of Quality; whose Favours as I am proud of, I shall always be industrious to preserve.

My Lord, I know the Respect and Reverence which in this Address I ought to appear in before You, who are so intimate with the Ancients, so general a Knower of the several Species of Poetry, and so Just a Judge in the Trials of this kind. You have an Absolute Power to Arraign and Convict, but a prevailing Inclination to Pardon and Save; and from the Humanity of Your Temper, and the true knowledge of the Difficulties of succeeding this way, never aggravate or insist upon Faults

> ——*Quas aut incuria fudit,*
> *Aut humana parùm cavit Natura*——
>
> Hor. Art. Poet.

to our Condemnation, where they are Venial, and not against the Principles of the Art we pretend to. *Horace*, who found it so, says,

> ——*Gratia Regum*
> *Pieriis tentata modis.*

The Favour of Great Men is the Poets Inheritance, and all Ages have allow'd 'em to put in their Claim; I only wish that I had Merit enough to prefer me to Your Grace: That I might deserve in some measure that Patronage which You are pleased to bestow on me: That I were a *Horace* for such a *Mecænas*. That I could describe what I admire; and tell the World what I really think, That as You possess those Infinite Advantages of Nature and Fortune in so Eminent a degree; that as You so far excel in the Perfections of Body and Mind, You were design'd and fashion'd a Prince, to be the Honour of the Nation, and the Grace and Ornament of the Court. *Sir*, In the Fulness of Happiness and Blessings which You enjoy, I can only bring in my Wishes for the Continuance of 'em; they shall constantly be devoted to you, with all the Services of,   M Y L O R D,

> *Your Grace's most Obliged, most*
> *Thankful, and most Humble Servant,*
>
> THO. SOUTHERNE.

PRO.

PROLOGUE to *Oroonoko.*

Sent by an Unknown Hand.   And Spoken by Mr. *Powell.*

AS when in *Hostile Times* two *Neighbouring States*
   Strive by *themselves,* and their *Confederates :*
   The *War* at *first,* is made with *awkard Skill,*
   And *Soldiers* clumfily each other *kill:*
Till time at length their *untaught Fury* tames,
And into *Rules* their heedless *Rage* reclaims :
Then every *Science* by degrees is made
Subfervient to the *Man-destroying Trade :*
Wit, Wisdom, Reading, Observation, Art ;
A well-turn'd *Head* to guide a *Generous Heart.*
So it may prove with our *Contending Stages,*
If you will kindly but fupply their *Wages :*
Which you with eafe may furnifh, by retrenching
Your *Superfluities* of *Wine* and *Wenching.*
Who'd grudge to fpare from *Riot* and hard *Drinking,*
To lay it out on means to mend his thinking ?
To follow fuch *Advice* you fhou'd have leifure,
Since what refines your *Senfe,* refines your *Pleafure :*
Women grown tame by *Ufe* each *Fool* can get,
But *Cuckolds* all are made by *Men of Wit.*
To *Virgin Favours Fools* have no pretence :
For *Maidenheads* were made for *Men of Senfe.*
'Tis not enough to have a *Horfe* well bred,
To fhew his *Mettle,* he muft be well fed :
Nor is it all in *Provender* and *Breed,*
He muft be try'd and ftrain'd, to mend his fpeed :
A *Favour'd Poet,* like a *Pamper'd Horfe,*
Will ftrain his *Eye-balls* out to win the *Courfe.*
Do you but in your *Wifdoms* vote it fit
To yield due *Succours* to this *War of Wit,*
The *Buskin* with more grace fhall tread the *Stage,*
Love figh in fofter *Strains,* *Heroes* lefs *Rage :*
Satyr fhall fhow a *Triple Row* of *Teeth,*
And *Comedy* fhall laugh your *Fops* to death :
Wit fhall refine, and *Pegafus* fhall fome,
And foar in fearch of *Ancient* Greece and Rome.
And fince the *Nation's* in the *Conquering Fit,*
As you by *Arms,* we'll vanquifh France *in Wit :*
The *Work* were over, cou'd our *Poets* write
With half the *Spirit* that our *Soldiers* fight.

B P H

EPILOGUE,

Written by Mr. *Congreve,* and Spoken by Mrs. *Verbruggen*

YOU see, we try all Shapes, and Shifts, and Arts,
 To tempt your Favours, and regain your Hearts.
We weep, and laugh, joyn mirth and grief together,
Like Rain and Sunshine mixt, in April weather.
Your different tasts divide our Poet's Cares:
One foot the Sock, t'other the Buskin wears:
Thus, while he strives to please, he's forc'd to do't,
Like Volscius, hip-hop, in a single Boot.
Criticks, he knows, for this may damn his Books:
But he makes Feasts for Friends, and not for Cooks.
Tho' Errant-Knights of late no favour find,
Sure you will be to Ladies-Errant kind.
To follow Fame, Knights-Errant make profession:
We Damsels flye, to save our Reputation:
So they, their Valour show, we, our Discretion.
To Lands of Monsters, and fierce Beasts they go:
We, to those Islands, where Rich Husbands grow:
Tho' they're no Monsters, we may make 'em so.
If they're of English growth, they'll bear't with patience:
But save us from a Spouse of *Oroonoko's* Nations!
Then bless your Stars, you happy London Wives,
Who love at large, each day, yet keep your lives:
Nor envy poor *Imoinda's* doating blindness,
Who thought her Husband kill'd her out of kindness.
Death with a Husband ne'er had shewn such Charms,
Had she once dy'd within a Lover's Arms.
Her error was from ignorance proceeding:
Poor Soul! she wanted some of our Town-Breeding.
Forgive this Indians fondness of her Spouse;
Their Law no Christian Liberty allows:
Alas! they make a Conscience of their Vows!
If Virtue in a Heathen be a fault;
Then Damn the Heathen School, where she was taught.
She might have learn'd to Cuckold, Jilt, and Sham,
Had Covent-Garden been in Surinam.

OROONOKO.

ACT I. SCENE I.

Enter Welldon *following* Lucia.

Luc. WHAT will this come to? What can it end in? You have perfuaded me to leave dear *England*, and dearer *London*, the place of the World moſt worth living in, to follow you a Husband-hunting into *America*: I thought Husbands grew in theſe Plantations.

Well. Why ſo they do, as thick as Oranges, ripening one under another. Week after Week they drop into ſome Woman's mouth: 'Tis but a little patience, ſpreading your Apron in expectation, and one of 'em will fall into your Lap at laſt.

Luc. Ay, ſo you ſay indeed.

Well. But you have left dear *London*, you ſay: Pray what have you left in *London* that was very dear to you, that had not left you before?

Luc. Speak for your ſelf, Siſter.

Well. Nay, I'll keep you in countenance. The Young Fellows, you know, the deareſt part of the Town, and without whom *London* had been a Wilderneſs to you and me, had forſaken us a great while.

Luc. Forſaken us! I don't know that they ever had us.

Well. Forſaken us the worſt way, Child; that is, did not think us worth having; they neglected us, no longer deſign'd upon us, they were tir'd of us. Women in *London* are like the Rich Silks, they are out of Faſhion a great while before they wear out. ——

Luc. The Devil take the Faſhion, I ſay.

Well. You may tumble 'em over and over at their firſt coming up, and never diſparage their Price; but they fall upon wearing immediately, lower and lower in their value till they come to the Broker at laſt.

Luc. Ay, ay, that's the Merchant they deal with. The Men would have us at their own ſcandalous Rates: Their Plenty makes 'em wanton; and in a little time, I ſuppoſe, they won't know what they would have of the Women themſelves.

Well. O, yes, they know what they wou'd have. They wou'd have a Woman give the Town a Pattern of her Perſon and Beauty, and not ſtay in it ſo long to have the whole Piece worn out. They wou'd have the good Face only diſcover'd, and not the Folly that commonly goes along with it. They ſay there is a vaſt Stock of Beauty in the Nation, but a great part of it lies in unprofitable hands; therefore for the good of the Publick, they wou'd have a Draught made once a Quarter, ſend the decaying Beauties for Breeders into the Country, to make room for New Faces to appear, to countenance the Pleaſures of the Town.

Luc. 'Tis very hard, the Men muſt be young as long as they live, and poor Women be thought decaying and unfit for the Town at One or Two and Twenty. I'm ſure we were not Seven Years in *London*.

VVell.

Well. Not half the time taken notice of, Sister. The Two or Three last Years we could make nothing of it, even in a Vizard-Masque; not in a Vizard-Masque, that has cheated many a man into an old acquaintance. Our Faces began to be as familiar to the Men of Intrigue, as their Duns, and as much avoided. We durst not appear in Publick Places, and were almost grudg'd a Gallery in the Churches: Even there they had their Jests upon us, and cry'd, She's in the right on't, good Gentlewoman, since no man considers her Body, she does very well indeed to take care of her Soul.

Luc. Such unmannerly Fellows there will always be.

Well. Then, you may remember, we were reduc'd to the last necessity, the necessity of making silly Visits to our civil Acquaintance, to bring us into tolerable Company. Nay, the young Inns-of-Court Beaus, of but one Term's standing in the Fashion, who knew no body, but as they were shewn 'em by the Orange-Women, had Nicknames for us: How often have they laugh'd out, There goes my Landlady; Is not she come to let Lodgings yet?

Luc. Young Coxcombs that knew no better.

Well. And that we must have come to. For your part, what Trade cou'd you set up in? You wou'd never arrive at the Trust and Credit of a Guinea-Bawd: You wou'd have too much Business of your own, ever to mind other Peoples.

Luc. That is true indeed.

Well. Then, as a certain sign that there was nothing more to be hop'd for, the Maids at the Chocolate Houses found us out, and laugh'd at us: Our *Billet-doux* lay there neglected for Waste-Paper: We were cry'd down so low we cou'd not pass upon the City; and became so notorious in our galloping way, from one end of the Town to t'other, that at last we cou'd hardly compass a competent change of Petticoats to disguise us to the Hackney-Coachmen: And then it was near walking a-foot indeed.

Luc. Nay, that I began to be afraid of.

Well. To prevent which, with what Youth and Beauty was left, some Experience, and the small Remainder of Fifteen hundred Pounds apiece, which amounted to bare Two hundred between us both, I persuaded you to bring your Person for a Venture to the *Indies*. Every thing has succeeded in our Voyage: I pass for your Brother; One of the Richest Planters here happening to dye just as we landed, I have claim'd Kindred with him; So, without making his Will, he has left us the Credit of his Relation to trade upon; We pass for his Cousins, coming here to *Surinam* chiefly upon his Invitation; We live in Reputation; have the best Acquaintance of the place; and we shall see our account in't, I warrant you.

Luc. I must rely upon you——

Enter Widow Lackitt.

Wid. Mr. *Welldon,* your Servant. Your Servant, Mrs. *Lucy.* I am an ill Visitor, but 'tis not too late, I hope, to bid you welcome to this side of the World.   [*Salutes* Lucy.

Well. Gad so, I beg your Pardon, Widow, I shou'd have done the Civilities of my House before; but, as you say, 'tis not too late, I hope——
                                        [*Going to kiss her.*
                                                        Wid.

Wid. What! You think now this was a Civil way of begging a Kiss; and by my Troth, if it were, I see no harm in't; 'tis a pitiful favour indeed that is not worth asking for: Though I have known a Woman speak plainer before now, and not understood neither.

Well. Not under my Roof. Have at you, Widow.——

Wid. Why, that's well said, spoke like a Younger Brother, that deserves to have Widow.—— [*He kisses her.*
You're a Younger Brother, I know, by your kissing.

Well. How so, pray?

Wid. Why, you kiss as if you expected to be paid for't. You have Birdlime upon your Lips. You stick so close, there's no getting rid of you.

Well. I am a kin to a Younger Brother.

Wid. So much the better: We Widows are commonly the better for Younger Brothers.

Luc. Better, or worse, most of you. But you won't be much better for him, I can tell you.—— [*aside.*

Well. I was a Younger Brother; but an Uncle of my Mother's has maliciously left me an Estate, and I'm afraid, spoil'd my Fortune.

Wid. No, no; an Estate will never spoil your Fortune; I have a good Estate my self, thank Heaven, and a kind Husband that left it behind him.

Well. Thank Heaven, that took him away from it, Widow, and left you behind him.

Wid. Nay, Heaven's will must be done; he's in a better place.

Well. A better place for you, no doubt on't: Now you may look about you; chuse for your self, Mrs. *Lackitt*, that's your business; for I know you design to marry again.

Wid. O dear! not I, I protest and swear; I don't design it: But I won't swear neither; one does not know what may happen to tempt one.

Well. Why, a lusty young Fellow may happen to tempt you.

Wid. Nay, I'll do nothing rashly: I'll resolve against nothing. The Devil, they say, is very busy upon these occasions; especially with the Widows. But if I am to be tempted, it must be with a Young Man, I promise you—— Mrs. *Lucy*, Your Brother is a very pleasant Gentleman: I came about Business to him, but he turns every thing into Merriment.

Well. Business, Mrs. *Lackitt*. Then, I know you wou'd have me to your self. Pray leave us together, Sister. [*Exit Lucia.*
What am I drawing upon my self here? [*Aside.*

Wid. You have taken a very pretty House here; every thing so neat about you already. I hear you are laying out for a Plantation.

Well. Why, yes truly, I like the Country, and wou'd buy a Plantation, if I cou'd reasonably.

Wid. O! by all means, reasonably.

Well. If I cou'd have one to my mind, I wou'd think of setling among you.

Wid. O! you can't do better. Indeed we can't pretend to have so good company for you, as you had in *England*; but we shall make very much of you. For my own part, I assure you, I shall think my self very happy to be more particularly known to you.

Wel.

VVell. Dear Mrs. *Lackitt*, you do me too much Honour.

VVid. Then as to a Plantation, Mr. *VVelldon*, you know I have several to dispose of. Mr. *Lackitt*, I thank him, has left me, though I say it, the Richest Widow upon the place; therefore I may afford to use you better than other people can. You shall have one upon any reasonable terms.

VVell. That's a fair Offer indeed.

VVid. You shall find me as easy as any body you can have to do with, I assure you. Pray try me, I wou'd have you try me, Mr. *VVelldon.* Well, I like that Name of yours exceedingly, Mr. *VVelldon.*

VVell. My Name!

VVid. O exceedingly! If any thing cou'd perswade me to alter my own Name, I verily believe nothing in the world wou'd do it so soon, as to be call'd Mrs. *VVelldon.*

VVell. Why, indeed *VVelldon* does sound something better than *Lackitt.*

VVid. O! a great deal better. Not that there is so much in a Name neither. But I don't know, there is something; I shou'd like mightily to be call'd Mrs. *VVelldon.*

VVell. I'm glad you like my Name.

VVid. Of all things. But then there's the misfortune, one can't change ones Name, without changing ones Condition.

VVell. You'l hardly think it worth that, I believe.

Wid. Think it worth what, Sir, Changing my Condition? Indeed, Sir, I think it worth every thing. But, alas! Mr. *VVelldon,* I have been a Widow but Six Months; 'tis too soon to think of changing ones Condition yet; indeed it is: Pray don't desire it of me: Not but that you may perswade me to any thing, sooner than any person in the world.———

VVell. Who, I, Mrs *Lackitt.*

VVid. Indeed you may, Mr. *VVelldon,* sooner than any man living. Lord, there's a great deal in saving a Decency: I never minded it before: Well, I'm glad you spoke first to excuse my Modesty. But what, Modesty means nothing, and is the Virtue of a Girl, that does not know what she would be at: A Widow should be wiser. Now will I own to you; but I wont confess neither; I have had a great Respect for you a great while: I beg your Pardon, Sir, and I must declare to you, indeed I must, if you desire to dispose of all I have in the world, in an Honourable Way, which I don't pretend to be any way deserving your consideration, my Fortune and Person, if you won't understand me without telling you so, are both at your service. Gad so another time———

Stanmore *enters to 'em.*

Stan. So, Mrs. *Lackitt,* your Widowhood is waneing apace, I see which way 'tis going. *Welldon,* you're a happy man. The Women and their Favours come home to you.

VVid. A fiddle of favour, Mr. *Stanmore:* I am a lone Woman, you know I left in a great deal of Business; and Business must be followed or lost. I have several Stocks and Plantations upon my hands, and other things to dispose of which Mr. *VVelldon* may have occasion for.

VVell. We were just upon the brink of a Bargain, as you came in.

Stan. Let me drive it on for you.

Well. So you muft, I believe, you or fomebody for me.

Stan. I'll ftand by you: I underftand more of this bufinefs, than you can pretend to.

Well. I don't pretend to't; 'tis quite out of my way indeed.

Stan. If the Widow gets you to her felf, fhe will certainly be too hard for you: I know her of old: She has no Confcience in a Corner; a very *Jew* in a bargain, and would circumcife you to get more of you.

Well. Is this true, Widow?

Wid. Speak as you find, Mr. *Welldon:* I have offer'd you very fair: Think upon't, and let me hear of you: The fooner the better, Mr. *Well-don.* ——— [*Exit.*

Stan. I affure you, my Friend, fhe'll cheat you if fhe can.

Well. I don't know that; but I can cheat her, if I will.

Stan. Cheat her? How?

Well. I can marry her; and then I'm fure I have it in my power to cheat her.

Stan. Can you marry her?

Well. Yes, faith, fo fhe fays: Her pretty Perfon and Fortune (which one, with the other, you know, are not contemptible) are both at my fervice.

Stan. Contemptible! very confiderable, I'gad; very defirable: Why, fhe's worth Ten thoufand Pounds, man; a clear Eftate: No charge upon't, but a boobily Son: He indeed was to have half; but his Father begot him, and fhe breeds him up, not to know or have more than fhe has a mind to; And fhe has a mind to fomething elfe, it feems.

Well. There's a great deal to be made of this. ——— *mufing.*

Stan. A handfome Fortune may be made on't; and I advife you to't, by all means.

Well. To marry her! an old, wanton Witch! I hate her.

Stan. No matter for that. Let her go to the Devil for you. She'll cheat her Son of a good Eftate for you; That's a Perquifite of a Widow's Portion always.

Well. I have a defign, and will follow her at leaft, till I have a Pen'worth of the Plantation.

Stan. I fpeak as a friend, when I advife you to marry her. For 'tis directly againft the Intereft of my own Family. My Coufin *Jack* has belabour'd her a good while that way.

Well. What! Honeft *Jack*! I'll not hinder him, I'll give over the thoughts of her.

Stan. He'll make nothing on't; fhe does not care for him. I'm glad you have her in your power.

Well. I may be able to ferve him.

Stan. Here's a Ship come into the River; I was in hopes it had been from England.

Well. From *England!*

Stan. No, I was difappointed; I long to fee this handfome Coufin of yours. The Picture you gave me of her has charm'd me.

Well. You'll fee whether it has flatter'd her or no, in a little time. If fhe recover'd of that Illnefs that was the reafon of her ftaying behind us, I know fhe will come with the firft opportunity. We fhall fee her, or hear of her death.

Stan.

Stan. We'll hope the beft. The Ships from *England* are expected every day.

Well. What Ship is this?

Stan. A Rover, a Buccaneer, a Trader in Slaves; That's the Commodity we deal in, you know. If you have a curiofity to fee our manner of marketing, I'll wait for you.

Well. We'll take my Sifter with us.——

[*Exeunt.*

SCENE II. *An Open Place*

Enter Lieutenant-Governor *and* Blanford

Gov. There's no refifting your Fortune, *Blanford*; you draw all the Prizes.

Blan. I draw for our Lord Governour, you know; his Fortune favours me.

Gov. I grudge him nothing this time; but if Fortune had favour'd me in the laft Sale, the Fair Slave had been mine; *Clemene* had been mine.

Blan. Are you ftill in love with her?

Gov. Every day more in love with her.

Enter Capt. Driver, *teaz'd and pull'd about by Widow* Lackitt *and feveral Planters. Enter at another door* Welldon, Lucia, Stanmore.

Wid. Here have I fix Slaves in my Lot, and not a Man among 'em; all Women and Children; what can I do with 'em, Captain? Pray confider I am a Woman my felf, and can't get my own Slaves, as fome of my Neighbours do.

1 Plan. I have all Men in time; Pray, Captain, let the Men and Women be mingled together, for Procreation-fake, and the good of the Plantation.

2 Plan. Ay, ay, a Man and a Woman, Captain, for the good of the Plantation.

Capt. Let 'em mingle together and be damn'd, what care I? Would you have me pimp for the good of the Plantation?

1 Plan. I am a conftant Cuftomer, Captain.

Wid. I am always Ready Money to you, Captain.

1 Plan. For that matter, Miftrefs, my Money is as ready as yours.

Wid. Pray hear me, Captain.

Capt. Look you, I have done my part by you; I have brought the number of Slaves you bargain'd for; if your Lots have not pleas'd you, you muft draw again among your felves.

3 Plan. I am contented with my Lot.

4 Plan. I am very well fatisfied.

5 Plan. We'll have no drawing again.

Capt. Do you hear, Miftrefs? You may hold your tongue. For my part I expect my Money.

Wid. Captain, No body queftions or fcruples the Payment. But I won't hold my tongue, 'tis too much to pray and pay too. One may fpeak for one's own I hope.

Capt. Well, what wou'd you fay?

Wid. I fay no more than I can make out.

Capt. Out with it then.

Wid. I fay, things have not been fo fair carry'd as they might have been. How do I know how you have juggled together in my abfence? You drew the Lots before I came, I'm fure.

Capt.

Capt. That's your own fault, Miftrefs ; you might have come fooner.

VVid. Then here's a Prince, as they fay, among the Slaves, and you fet him down to go as a common Man.

Capt. Have you a mind to try what a Man he is ? You'll find him no more than a common Man at your bufinefs.

VVid. Sir, You're a fcurvy Fellow to talk at this rate to me. If my Huf-band were alive, Gadsbodykins, you wou'd not ufe me fo.

Capt. Right, Miftrefs, I would not ufe you at all.

VVid. Not ufe me! Your Betters every Inch of you, I wou'd have you to know, wou'd be glad to ufe me, Sirrah. Marry come up here, who are you, I trow ? You begin to think your felf a Captain, forfooth, becaufe we call you fo. You forget your felf as faft as you can ; but I remember you ; I know you for a pitiful paltry Fellow, as you are ; an Upftart to Profperity ; one that is but juft come acquainted with Cleanlinefs, and that never faw Five Shillings of your own, without deferving to be hang'd for 'em.

Gov. She has giv'n you a Broadfide, Captain ; You'll ftand up to her.

Capt. Hang her, Stink-pot, I'll come no nearer.

VVid. By this good light, it wou'd make Woman do a thing fhe ne-ver defign'd ; Marry again, tho fhe were fure to repent it, to be reveng'd of fuch a ——

J. Stan. What's the matter, Mrs. *Lackitt* ? Can I ferve you ?

VVid. No, no, you can't ferve me: You are for ferving your felf, I'm fure. Pray go about your bufinefs, I have none for you : You know I have told you fo. Lord ! how can you be fo troublefome ? nay, fo unconfcionable, to think that every Rich Widow muft throw her felf away upon a Young Fellow that has nothing ?

Stan. *Jack*, You are anfwer'd, I fuppofe,

J. Stan. I'll have another pluck at her.

VVid. Mr.*VVelldon*, I am a little out of order : but pray bring your Sifter to dine with me. Gad's my life, I'm out of all patience with that pitiful Fellow : My Flefh rifes at him: I can't ftay in the place where he is. —— [*Exit.*

Elan. Captain, You have us'd the Widow very familiarly.

Capt. This is my way ; I have no defign, and therefore am not over civil. If fhe had ever a handfome Daughter to wheedle her out of: Or if I cou'd make any thing of her Booby Son.

Well. I may improve that hint, and make fomething of him. [*afide.*

Gov. She's very Rich.

Capt. I'm rich my felf. She has nothing that I want. I have no Leaks to ftop. Old Women are Fortune-Menders. I have made a good Voyage, and wou'd reap the fruits of my labour. We plow the deep, my Mafters, but our Harveft is on fhore. I'm for a Young Woman.

Stan. Look about, Captain, there's one ripe, and ready for the Sickle.

Capt. A Woman indeed ! I will be acquainted with her: Who is fhe ?

Well. My Sifter, Sir.

Capt. Wou'd I were a-kin to her: If fhe were my Sifter, fhe fhou'd never go out of the Family. What fay you, Miftrefs ? You expect I fhould marry you, I fuppofe ?

Luc. I fhan't be difappointed, if you don't. [*turning away.*

Well. She won't break her heart, Sir. *Capt,*

Capt. But I mean————   [*following her.*

Well. And I mean ————   [*Going between him and Lucia.*

That you muſt not think of her without marrying.

Capt. I mean ſo too.

Well. Why then your meaning's out.

Capt. You're very ſhort.

Well. I will grow, and be taller for you.

Capt. I ſhall grow angry, and ſwear.

Well. You'll catch no Fiſh then.

Capt. I don't well know whether he deſigns to affront me, or no.

Stan. No, no, he's a little familiar ; 'tis his way.

Capt. Say you ſo? Nay, I can be as familiar as he, if that be it. Well, Sir, look upon me full ; What ſay you? How do you like me for a Brother-in-Law?

Well. Why yes , faith, you'll do my Buſineſs, [*turning him about.*] If we can agree about my Siſter's.

Capt. I don't know whether your Siſter will like me, or not ; I can't ſay much to her ; But I have Money enough ; And if you are her Brother, as you ſeem to be a-kin to her, I know that will recommend me to you.

Well. This is your Market for Slaves ; my Siſter is a Free Woman, and muſt not be diſpos'd of in publick. You ſhall be welcome to my Houſe, if you pleaſe ; And upon better acquaintance, if my Siſter likes you, and I like your Offers,——

Capt. Very well, Sir, I'll come and ſee her.

Gov. Where are the Slaves, Captain? They are long a coming.

Blan. And who is this Prince that's fallen to my Lot, for the Lord Governor? Let me know ſomething of him, that I may treat him accordingly ; who is he?

Capt. He's the Devil of a Fellow , I can tell you ; a Prince every Inch of him : You have paid dear enough for him, for all the good he'll do you : I was forc'd to clap him in Irons, and did not think the Ship ſafe neither. You are in hoſtility with the *Indians*, they ſay ; they threaten you daily : You had beſt have an Eye upon him.

Blan. But who is he?

Gov. And how do you know him to be a Prince?

Capt. He is Son and Heir to the great King of *Angola*, a miſchievous Monarch in thoſe parts, who, by his good will , wou'd never let any of his Neighbours be in quiet. This Son was his General, a plaguy fighting Fellow ; I have formerly had dealings with him for Slaves, which he took Priſoners, and have got pretty roundly by him. But the Wars being at an end, and nothing more to be got by the Trade of that Country, I made bold to bring the Prince along with me.

Gov. How could you do that?

Blan. What! ſteal a Prince out of his own Country? Impoſſible!

Capt. 'Twas hard indeed ; but I did it. You muſt know, this *Oroonoko*.———

Blan. Is that his Name?

Ay, *Oroonoko*.

Gov. *Oroonoko*.

                                            Capt.

Capt. Is naturally Inquifitive about the Men and Manners of the White Nations. Becaufe I could give him fome account of the other Parts of the World, I grew very much into his favour ; In return of fo great an Honour, you know I cou'd do no lefs upon my coming away, than to invite him on board me; Never having been in a Ship, he appointed his time, and I prepared my Entertainment ; He came the next Evening as privately as he cou'd, with about fome Twenty along with him. The Punch went round ; and as many of his Attendants as wou'd be dangerous, I fent dead drunk on fhore; the reft we fecur'd ; And fo you have the Prince *Oroonoko*.

1 Plan. Gad-a-mercy, Captain, there you were with him, I'faith.

2 Plan. Such men as you are fit to be employ'd in Publick Affairs ; The Plantation will thrive by you.

3 Plan. Induftry fhou'd be encourag'd.

Capt. There's nothing done without it, Boys. I have made my Fortune this way.

Blan. Unheard of Villany !

Stan. Barbarous Treachery !

Blan. They applaud him for't.

Gov. But, Captain , Methinks you have taken a great deal of pains for this Prince *Oroonoko* ; why did you part with him at the common rate of Slaves ?

Capt. Why, Lieutenant-Governor, I'll tell you ; I did defign to carry him to *England,* to have fhow'd him there ; but I found him troublefome upon my hands, and I'm glad I'm rid of him.——Oh, ho, here they come.

Black Slaves, Men, Women, and Children, pafs acrofs the Stage by two and two ; Aboan , and others of Oroonoko's *Attendants two and two ;* Oroonoko *laft of all in Chains.*

Luc. Are all thefe Wretched Slaves ?

Stan. All fold, they and their Pofterity all Slaves.

Luc. O miferable Fortune !

Blan. Moft of 'em know no better ; they were born fo, and only change their Mafters. But a Prince, born only to Command, betray'd and fold ! My heart drops blood for him.

Capt. Now, Governor, here he comes, pray obferve him.

Oro. So, Sir, You have kept your word with me.

Capt. I am a better Chriftian, I thank you, than to keep it with a Heathen.

Oro. You are a Chriftian, be a Chriftian ftill ;
If you have a God that teaches you
To break your word, I need not curfe you more ;
Let him cheat you, as you are falfe to me.
You faithful Followers of my better Fortune !
We have been Fellow-Soldiers in the Field ;   [*Embracing his Friends*.
Now we are Fellow-Slaves. This laft Farewel.
Be fure of one thing that will comfort us,
Whatever World we next are thrown upon,
Cannot be worfe than this.   *All Slaves go off, but* Oroonoko.

Capt. You fee what a Bloody Pagan he is, Governor ; but I took care that
none

none of his Followers fhould be in the fame Lot with him, for fear they
fhou'd undertake fome defperate action, to the danger of the Colony.

Oro. Live ftill in fear ; it is the Villains Curfe,
And will revenge my Chains : Fear ev'n me,
Who have no power to hurt thee.   Nature abhors,
And drives thee out from the Society
And Commerce of Mankind for Breach of Faith.
Men live and profper but in mutual Truft,
A Confidence of one another's Truth ;
That thou haft violated.   I have done.
I know my Fortune, and fubmit to it.

Gov. I am forry for your Fortune, and wou'd help it, if I cou'd.

Blan. Take off his Chains.   You know your condition ; but you are fal'n
into Honourable Hands ; You are the Lord Governor's Slave, who will ufe
you nobly ; In his abfence it fhall be my care to ferve you.   [*Blandford*

Oro. I hear you, but I can believe no more.   *applying to him.*

Gov. Captain, I'm afraid the world won't fpeak fo honourably of this
action of yours, as you wou'd have 'em.

Capt. I have the Money.   Let the world fpeak and be damn'd, I care not.

Oro. I wou'd forget my felf.   Be fatisfied,   [*to Blandford,*
I am above the rank of common Slaves.
Let that content you.   The Chriftian there, that knows me,
For his own fake will not difcover more.

Capt. I have other matters to mind.   You have him, and much good may
do you with your Prince.   [*Exit.*

The Planters pulling and ftaring at Oroonoko.

Blan. What wou'd you have there ? You ftare as if you never faw a Man
before.   Stand further off.   [*turns 'em away.*

Oro. Let 'em ftare on. I am unfortunate, but not afham'd
Of being fo : No, let the Guilty blufh,
The White Man that betray'd me : Honeft Black
Difdains to change its Colour.   I am ready ;
Where muft I go ? Difpofe me as you pleafe.
I am not well acquainted with my Fortune,
But muft learn to know it better. So I know, you fay,
Degrees make all things eafy.

Blan. All things fhall be eafy.

Oro. Tear off this Pomp, and let me know my felf.
The flavifh Habit beft becomes me now.
Hard Fare, and Whips, and Chains may overpow'r
The frailer Flefh, and bow my Body down.
But there's another, Nobler Part of Me,
Out of your reach, which you can never tame.

Blan. You fhall find nothing of this wretchednefs
You apprehend.   We are not Monfters all.
You feem unwilling to difclofe your felf ;
Therefore for fear the mentioning your Name
Should give you new difquiets, I prefume
To call you *Cefar.*

Oro. I am my self; but call me what you please.

Stan. A very good Name, *Cæsar.*

Gov. And very fit for his great Character.

Oro. Was *Cæsar* then a Slave?

Gov. I think he was; to Pyrates too; he was a great Conqueror, but unfortunate in his Friends.——

Oro. His Friends were Christians?

Blan. No.

Oro. No! that's strange.

Gov. And murder'd by 'em.

Oro. I wou'd be *Cæsar* there; yet I will live.

Blan. Live to be happier.

Oro. Do what you will with me.

Blan. I'll wait upon you, attend, and serve you.   [*Exit with* Oroonoko.

Luc. Well, if the Captain had brought this Prince's Country along with him, and wou'd make me Queen of it, I wou'd not have him, after doing so base a thing.

Well. He's a Man to thrive in the world, Sister; he'll make you the better Jointure.

Luc. Hang him, nothing can prosper with him.

Stan. Enquire into the great Estates, and you will find most of 'em depend upon the same Title of Honesty. The men who raise 'em first are much of the Captain's Principles.

Well. Ay, ay, as you say, let him be damn'd for the good of his Family. Come, Sister, we are invited to dinner.

Gov. Stanmore, You dine with me.   [*Exeunt omnes.*

A C T II. Scene I. *Widow* Lackitt's *House.*

Widow Lackitt, Welldon.

Well. THis is so great a Favour, I don't know how to receive it.

Wid. O dear Sir! you know how to receive and how to return a Favour, as well as any body, I don't doubt it. 'Tis not the first you have had in our Sex, I suppose.

Well. But this is so unexpected.

Wid. Lord, how can you say so, Mr. *Welldon?* I won't believe you. I know you handsome Gentlemen expect every thing that a Woman can do for you? And by my troth you're in the right on't. I think one can't do too much for a Handsome Gentleman; and so you shall find it.

Well. I shall never have such an Offer again, that's certain; What shall I do? I am mightily divided ———   [*pretending a concern.*

Wid. Divided! O dear, I hope not so, Sir. If I marry, truly I expect to have you to my self.

Well. There's no danger of that, Mrs. *Lackitt.* I am divided in my thoughts. My Father upon his Death bed oblig'd me to see my Sister dispos'd of, before I married my self. 'Tis that sticks upon me. They say indeed Promises are

C   to to be broken or kept ; and I know 'tis a foolish thing to be tied to a Promife; but I can't help it ; I don't know how to get rid of it.

Wid. Is that all ?

Well. All in all to me. The Commands of a dying Father , you know, ought to be obey'd.

Wid. And fo they may.

Well. Impoffible, to do me any good.

Wid. They fhan't be your hindrance. You wou'd have a Husband for your Sifter. you fay : He muft be very well to pafs too in the world, I fuppofe?

Well. I wou'd not throw her away.

VVid. Then marry her out of hand to the Sea-Captain you were fpeaking of.

VVell. I was thinking of him, but 'tis to no purpofe: She hates him.

VVid. Does fhe hate him? Nay, 'tis no matter, an impudent Rafcal as he is, I wou'd not advife her to marry him.

VVell. Can you think of no body elfe ?

VVid. Let me fee.

VVell. Ay, pray do ; I fhou'd be loth to part with my good fortune in you for fo fmall a matter as a Sifter. But you find how it is with me.

VVid. Well remembred, i'faith. Well, if I thought you wou'd like of it, I have a Husband for her ; What do you think of my Son ?

VVell. You don't think of it your felf.

VVid. I proteft but I do ; I am in earneft, if you are. He fhall marry her within this half hour, if you'll give your confent to it.

VVell. I give my confent ! I'll anfwer for my Sifter, fhe fhall have him. You may be fure I fhall be glad to get over the difficulty.

KVid. No more to be faid then, that difficulty is over. But I vow and fwear you frightned me, Mr. *VVelldon.* If I had not had a Son now for your Sifter, what muft I have done do you think? Were not you an ill-natur'd thing to boggle at a Promife? I cou'd break twenty for you.

VVell. I am the more oblig'd to you.: But this Son will fave all.

VVid. He's in the Houfe, I'll go and bring him my felf. *[going* You wou'd do well to break the bufinefs to your Sifter. She's within, I'll fend her to you.—— *[going again, comes back*

VVell. Pray do.

VVid. But d'you hear? Perhaps fhe may ftand upon her Maidenly Behavi-our, and blufh, and play the fool, and delay. But don't be anfwer'd fo, What ! fhe is not a Girl at thefe years: Shew your Authority, and tell her roundly, fhe muft be married immediately. I'll manage my Son, I warrant you.—— *[goes out in hafte.*

VVell. The Widow's in hafte, I fee. I thought I had laid a tub in the road about my Sifter: But fhe has ftept over that. She's making way for her felf as faft as fhe can ; but little thinks where fhe is going. I cou'd tell her fhe's going to play the fool. But people don't love to hear of their faults ; Befides that is not my bufinefs at prefent.

So, Sifter, I have a Husband for you.—— *[Enter Luci.*

Luc. With all my heart. I don't know what Confinement Marriage may be to the Men, but I'm fure the Women have no liberty without it. I am fo any thing that will deliver me from the care of a Reputation which I begin to find impoffible to preferve.

VVell

Well. I'll eafe you of that care: You muſt be married immediately.

Luc. The ſooner the better; for I am quite tir'd of ſetting up for a Huſ-band. The Widow's fooliſh Son is the man, I ſuppoſe.

Well. I confider'd your Conſtitution, Sifter; and finding you wou'd have occaſion for a Fool, I have provided accordingly.

Luc. I don't know what occaſion I may have for a Fool when I'm married But I find none but Fools have occaſion to marry.

Well. Since he is to be a Fool then, I thought it better for you to have one of his Mother's making than your own; 'twill ſave you the trouble.

Luc. I thank you; you take a great deal of pains for me: But pray tell me, what are you doing for your ſelf all this while.

Well. You were never true to your own ſecrets, and therefore I won't truſt you with mine. Only remember this, I am your elder Sifter, and conſequent-ly laying my Breeches aſide, have as much occaſion for a Husband as you can have. I have a man in my eye, be ſatisfied.

Enter *Widow* Lackit, *with her Son* Daniel.

Wid. Come, *Daniel*, hold up thy head, Child. Look like a Man: You muſt not take it as you have done. Gad's my life! there's nothing to be done with twirling your Hat, Man.

Dan. Why, Mother, what's to be done then?

Wid. Why look me in the face, and mind what I ſay to you.

Dan. Marry, who's the fool then, what ſhall I get by minding what you ſay to me?

Wid. Mrs. *Lucy*, the Boy is baſhful, don't diſcourage him; Pray come a lit-tle forward, and let him ſalute you.   [*Going between* Lucia *and* Daniel.

Luc. A fine Husband I am to have truly.   [*to* Welldon.

Wid. Come, *Daniel*, you muſt be acquainted with this Gentlewoman.

Dan. Nay, I'm not proud, that is not my fault; I am preſently acquaint-ed when I know the Company; but this Gentlewoman is a ſtranger to me.

Wid. She is your Miſtreſs; I have ſpoke a good word for you; make her a Bow, and go and kiſs her.

Dan. Kiſs her! Have a care what you ſay; I warrant ſhe ſcorns your words. Such Fine Folk are not us'd to be ſtopt and kiſs'd. Do you think I don't know that, Mother?

Wid. Try her, try her, Man.   [Daniel *bows, ſhe thruſts him forward.*
Why, that's well done, go nearer her.

Dan. Is the Devil in the Woman? Why, ſo I can go nearer her, if you would let a body alone.   [*To his Mother.*
Cry you mercy, forſooth; my Mother is always ſhaming one before company. She wou'd have me as unmannerly as her ſelf, and offer to kiſs you. [*To* Lucia.

Well. Why, won't you kiſs her?

Dan. Why, pray, may I?

Well. Kiſs her, kiſs her, Man.

Dan. Marry, and I will. [*Kiſſes her.*] Gadſooks! ſhe kiſſes rarely! An' pleaſe you, Miſtreſs, and ſeeing my Mother will have it ſo, I don't much care if I kiſs you again, forſooth.   [*Kiſſes her again.*

Luc. Well, how do you like me now.

Dan.

Dan. Like you? marry, I don't know. You have bewitch'd me, I think, I was never fo in my born days before.

VVid. You muft marry this Fine Woman, *Daniel.*

Dan. Hey day! marry her! I was never married in all my life. What muft I do with her then, Mother?

VVid. You muft live with her, eat and drink with her, go to bed with her, and fleep with her.

Dan. Nay, marry, if I muft go to bed with her, I fhall never fleep, that's certain. She'll break me of my reft, quite and clean, I tell you before-hand. As for eating and drinking with her, why I have a good ftomach, and can play my part in any company. But how do you think I can go to bed to a Woman I don't know?

VVell. You fhall know her better.

Dan. Say you fo, Sir?

VVell. Kifs her again.   [Daniel *kiffes* Lucy.

Dan. Nay, kiffing I find will make us prefently acquainted. We'll fteal into a Corner to practife a little, and then I fhall be able to do any thing.

VVell. The Young Man mends apace.

VVid. Pray don't baulk him.

Dan. Mother, Mother, if you'll ftay in the room by me, and promife not to leave me, I don't care for once if I venture to go to bed with her.

Wid. There's a good Child, go in and put on thy beft Cloaths; pluck up a fpirit; I'll ftay in the room by thee. She won't hurt thee, I warrant thee.

Dan. Nay, as to that matter, I'm not afraid of her. I'll give her as good as fhe brings; I have a *Rowland* for her *Oliver*, and fo you may tell her. [*Exit.*

Wid. Mrs. *Lucy*, we fhan't ftay for you. You are in readinefs, I fuppofe.

Well. She's always ready to do what I wou'd have her. I muft fay that for my Sifter.

Wid. 'Twill be her own another day. Mr. *Welldon*, we'll marry 'em out of hand, and then——

Well. And then, Mrs. *Lackitt*, look to your felf.——   [*Exeunt.*

S C E N E II.

Oroonoko *and* Blandford.

Oro. YOU grant I have good reafon to fufpect
All the profeffions you can make to me.

Blan. Indeed you have.——

Oro. The Dog that fold me did profefs as much
As you can do.——But yet I know not why;——
Whether it is becaufe I'm fall'n fo low,
And have no more to fear.——That is not it;
I am a Slave no longer than I pleafe.
'Tis fomething nobler.——Being juft my felf,
I am inclining to think others fo.
'Tis that prevails upon me to believe you.

Blan. You may believe me.

Oro. I do believe you.
From what I know of you, you are no Fool.
Fools only are the Knaves, and live by Tricks ;
Wife men may thrive without 'em, and be honeft.

    Blan. They won't all take your counfel. ———   [*Afide*

    Oro. You know my Story, and you fay you are
A Friend to my Misfortunes ; That's a name
Will teach you what you owe your felf and me.

    Blan. I'll ftudy to deferve to be your Friend,
When once our noble Governor arrives,
With him you will not need my Intereft ;
He is too generous not to feel your wrongs.
But be affur'd I will employ mÿ pow'r,
And find the means to fend you home again.

    Oro. I thank you, Sir.———My honeft, wretched Friends!   [*fighing.*
Their Chains are heavy ; they have hardly found
So kind a Mafter. May I ask you, Sir,
What is become of 'em ? Perhaps I fhou'd not.
You will forgive a Stranger.

    Blan. I'll enquire. and ufe my beft endeavours, where they are,
To have 'em gently u.'d.

    Oro. Once more I thank you.
You offer every Cordial that can keep
My Hopes alive, to wait a better day.
What Friendly Care can do, you have apply'd.
But, Oh ! I have a Grief admits no Cure.

    Blan. You do not know, Sir,——

    Oro. Can you raife the dead ?
Purfue and overtake the Wings of Time ?
And bring about again the Hours, the Days,
The years that made me happy.

    Blan. That Is not to be done.

    Oro. No, there is nothing to be done for me. [*Kneeling and Kiffing the Earth.*
Thou God ador'd ! thou ever-glorious Sun !
If fhe be yet on Earth, fend me a Beam
Of thy All-feeing Power to light me to her.
Or if thy Sifter Goddefs has prefer'd
Her Beauty to the Skies to be a Star ;
O tell me where fhe fhines, that I may ftand
Whole Nights, and gaze upon her.

    Blan. I am rude, and interrupt you.

    Oro. I am troublefome.
But pray give me your Pardon. My fwoll'n Heart
Burfts out its paffage, and I muft complain.
O! can you think of nothing dearer to me ?
Dearer than Liberty, my Country, Friends,
Much dearer than my Life ? That I have loft.
The tend'reft, beft belov'd, and loving Wife.

    Blan. Alas I pity you.   *Oro.*

Oro. Do, pity me;
Pity's a-kin to Love; and every thought
Of that soft kind is welcome to my Soul.
I wou'd be pity'd here.

Blan. I dare not ask more than you please to tell me; but if you
Think it convenient to let me know
Your Story, I dare promise you to bear
A part in your Distress, if not assist you.

Oro. Thou honest-hearted man! I wanted such,
Just such a Friend as thou art, that would sit
Still as the night, and let me talk whole days
Of my *Imoinda.* O! I'll tell thee all
From first to last; and pray observe me well.

Blan. I will most heedfully.

Oro. There was a Stranger in my Father's Court,
Valu'd and honour'd much. He was a White,
The first I ever saw of your Complexion.
He chang'd his gods for ours, and so grew great;
Of many Virtues, and so fam'd in Arms,
He still commanded all my Father's Wars.
I was bred under him. One Fatal Day,
The Armies joining, he before me stept,
Receiving in his Breast a Poison'd Dart
Levell'd at me; He dy'd within my Arms.
I've tir'd you already.

Blan. Pray go on.

Oro. He left an only Daughter, whom he brought
An Infant to *Angola.* When I came
Back to the Court, a happy Conqueror;
Humanity oblig'd me to condole
With this sad Virgin for a Father's Loss,
Lost for my safety. I presented her
With all the Slaves of Battel to atone
Her Father's Ghost. But when I saw her Face,
And heard her speak, I offer'd up my self
To be the Sacrifice. She bow'd and blush'd;
I wonder'd and ador'd. The Sacred Pow'r
That had subdu'd me, then inspir'd my Tongue,
Inclin'd her Heart; and all our Talk was Love.

Blan. Then you were happy.

Oro. O! I was too happy.
I marry'd her: And though my Countrey's Custom
Indulg'd the Privilege of many Wives,
I swore my self never to know but her.
She grew with Child, and I grew happier still.
O my *Imoinda*! but it cou'd not last.
Her fatal Beauty reach'd my Father's Ears;
He sent for her to Court, where, cursed Court!

No Woman comes, but for his Amorous Ufe.
He raging to poffefs her, fhe was forc'd
To own her felf my Wife. The furious King
Started at Inceft: But grown defperate,
Not daring to enjoy what he defir'd,
In mad Revenge, which I cou'd never learn,
He Poifon'd her, or.fent her far, far off,
Far from my hopes ever to fee her more.
   Blan. Moft barbarous of Fathers ! the fad Tale
Has ftruck me dumb with wonder.
   Oro. I have done.
i'll trouble you no farther ; now and then,
A Sigh will have its way; that fhall be all.
                  Enter Stanmore.
   Stan. Blanford, the Lieutenant Governor is gone to your Plantation.
He defires you wou'd bring the Royal Slave with you.
The fight of his fair Miftrefs, he fays, is an Entertainment
For a Prince ; he wou'd have his opinion of her.
   Oro. Is he a Lover ?
   Blan. So he fays himfelf ; he flatters a beautiful
Slave, that I have, and calls her Miftrefs.
   Oro. Muft he then flatter her, to call her Miftrefs ?
I pity the proud Man, who thinks himfelf
Above being in love ; what, tho' fhe be a Slave,
She may deferve him.
   Blan. You fhall judge of that, when you fee her, Sir,
   Oro. I go with you.
                                      [*Exeunt*

SCENE III. *A Plantation.*

[*L. Governor following* Imoinda.]

   Gov. I have difturb'd you. I confefs my fault,
My fair *Clemene,* but begin again,
And I will liften to your mournful Song,
Sweet as the foft complaining Nightingales.
While every Note calls out my trembling Soul,
And leaves me filent, as the Midnight Groves,
Only to fhelter you, fing, fing, agen,
And let me wonder at the many ways
You have to ravifh me.
   Imo. O ! I can weep
Enough for you, and me, if that will pleafe you.
   Gov. You muft not weep : I come to dry your Tears,
And raife you from your Sorrow. Look upon me:
Look with the Eyes of kind indulging Love,
That I may have full caufe for what I fay ;
I come to offer you your Liberty,
And be my felf the Slave. You turn away.
                                    [*Following her.*
                                           But

But every thing becomes you. I may take
This pretty hand : I know your Modesty
Wou'd draw it back : but you wou'd take it ill,
If I fhou'd let it go, I know you wou'd.
You fhall be gently forc'd to pleafe your felf ;
That you will thank me for.   [*She ftruggles, and gets her hand from him,*
Nay If you ftruggle with me, I muft take—— *then he offers to kifs her.*
  Imo. You may, my Life, that I can part with freely.   [*Exit.*
  [*Enter* Blandford, Stanmore, Oroonoko *to him.*]
  Blan. So, Governor, we don't difturb you, I hope : your Miftrefs has left
you : you were making Love, fhe's thankful for the Honour, I fuppofe.
  Gov. Quite infenfible to all I fay, and do ;
When I fpeak to her, fhe fighs, or weeps,
But never anfwers me as I wou'd have her.
  Stan. There's fomething nearer than her Slavery, that touches her.
  Blan. What do her fellow Slaves fay of her ? can't they find the caufe ?
  Gov. Some of 'em, who pretend to be wifer than the reft, and hate her,
I fuppofe, for being us'd better than they are, will needs have it that fhe's
with Child.
  Blan. Poor wretch ! if it be fo, I pity her :
She has loft a Husband, that perhaps was dear
To her ; then you cannot blame her.
  Oro. If it be fo, indeed you cannot blame her.   [*Sighing.*
  Gov. No, no, it is not fo : If it be fo,
I ftill muft love her : and defiring ftill,
I muft enjoy her.
  Blan. Try what you can do with fair means, and welcome.
  Gov. I'll give you ten Slaves for her.
  Blan. You know fhe is our Lord Governor's : but if I could Difpofe of her,
I wou'd not now, efpecially to you.
  Gov. Why not to me ?
  Blan. I mean againft her Will. You are in love with her,
And we all know what your defires wou'd have :
Love ftops at nothing but poffeffion.
Were fhe within your pow'r, you do not know
How foon you wou'd be tempted to forget
The Nature of the Deed, and, may be, act
A violence, you after wou'd repent
  Oro. 'Tis Godlike in you to protect the weak.
  Gov. Fye, fye, I wou'd not force her. Tho' fhe be
A Slave, her Mind is free, and fhou'd confent :
  Oro. Such Honour will engage her to confent :
And then, if you'r in love, fhe's worth the having.
Shall we not fee this wonder ?
  Gov. Have a care ?
You have a Heart, and fhe has conquering Eyes.
  Oro. I have a Heart ; but if it cou'd be falfe
To my firft Vows ever to love agen,
Thefe honeft Hands fhou'd tear it from my Breaft,

                              And

And throw the Traytor from me. O! *Imoinda!*
Living or dead, I can be only thine.
Blan. *Imoinda* was his Wife: she's either dead;
Or living, dead to him; forc'd from his Arms
By an inhuman Father. Another time
I'll tell you all. [*To* Gov. *and* Stanmore
Stan. Hark! the Slaves have done their work;
And now begins their Evening merriment.
Blan. The Men are all in love with fair *Clemene*
As much as you are; and the Women hate her,
From an instinct of natural jealousy.
They sing, and dance, and try their little tricks
To entertain her, and divert her sadness.
May be she is among 'em; shall we see? [*Exeunt.*

The Scene drawn shews the Slaves, Men, Women, and Children upon the Ground, some rise and dance, others sing the following Songs.

A SONG [By an unknown Hand.]
Set by Mr. *Courtevil*, and sung by the Boy to *Miss Cross.*

I.
A Lass there lives upon the Green,
  Cou'd I her Picture draw;
A brighter Nymph was never seen,
That looks, and reigns a little Queen,
  And keeps the Swains in awe.

II.
Her Eyes are Cupid's Darts and Wings,
  Her Eyebrows are his Bow;

Her Silken Hair the Silver Strings,
Which sure and swift destruction brings
  To all the Vale below.

III.
If Pastorella's dawning Light,
  Can warm, and wound us so:
Her Noon will shine so piercing bright,
Each glancing beam will kill outright,
  And every Swain subdue.

A SONG, By Mr. *Cheek.*
Set by Mr. *Courtevil*, and sung by Mr. *Leveridge.*

I.
Bright Cynthia's Pow'r divinely great,
  What Heart is not obeying?
A thousand Cupids on her wait,
  And in her Eyes are playing.

II.
She seems the Queen of Love to reign,
  For she alone dispences
Such Sweets as best can entertain
  The Gust of all the Senses.

III.
Her Face a charming Prospect brings;
  Her Breath gives balmy Blisses:
I hear an Angel when she sings,
  And taste of Heaven in Kisses.

IV.
Four Senses thus she Feasts with joy,
  From Nature's richest Treasure:
Let me the other Sense employ,
  And I shall dye with pleasure.

During the Entertainment, the Governor, Blanford, Stanmore, Oroonoko, enter as Spectators; that ended, Captain Driver, Jack Stanmore, and several Planters enter with their Swords drawn. [A Bell rings.

D   Capt.

Capt. Where are you, Governor? make what haste you can.
To save your self, and the whole Colony.
I bid 'em ring the Bell.

Gov. What's the matter?

J. Stan. The *Indians* are come down upon us:
They have plunder'd some of the Plantations already,
And are marching this way as fast as they can.

Gov. What can we do against 'em?

Blan. We shall be able to make a stand
Till more Planters come in to us.

J. Stan. There are a great many more without,
If you wou'd show your self, and put us in order.

Gov. There's no danger of the White Slaves, they'll not stir.
Blanford and *Stanmore* come you along with me:
Some of you stay here to look after the Black Slaves.

All go out but the Captain and 6 Planters, who all at once seize Oroonoko.

1. *Plan.* Ay, ay, let us alone.

Capt. In the first place we secure you, Sir,
As an Enemy to the Government.

Oro. Are you there, Sir, you are my constant Friend.

1. *Plan.* You will be able to do a great deal of mischief.

Capt. But we shall prevent you, bring the Irons hither.
He has the malice of a Slave in him, and wou'd be glad to be cutting his Masters
Throats, I know him. Chain his hands and feet, that he may not run over to
'em: if they have him, they shall carry him on their backs, that I can tell 'em.

[*As they are chaining him,* Blanford *enters, runs to 'em.*]

Blan. What are you doing there?

Capt. Securing the main chance. This is a bosom enemy.

Blan. Away you Brutes, I'll answer with my life for his behaviour; so tell
the Governor.

Capt. } Well, Sir, so we will.   { *Exeunt Capt. and*
Plan. }   {   *Planters.*

Oro. Give me a Sword, and I'll deserve your trust.

A Party of Indians *enter, hurrying* Imoinda *among the Slaves: another*
Party of Indians *sustains 'em retreating, followed at a distance by the Go-*
vernor with the Planters. Blanford, Oroonoko *joins 'em.*

Blan. Hell, and the Devil! they drive away our Slaves before our Face.
Governor, can you stand tamely by, and suffer this? *Clemene,* Sir, your Mistress is among 'em.

Gov. We throw our selves away, in the attempt to rescue 'em.

Oro. A Lover cannot fall more glorious
Than in the cause of Love. He that deserves
His Mistress's favour wonnot stay behind.
I'll lead you on, be bold, and follow me.

Oroonoko *at the head of the Planters falls upon the Indians with a great*
shout, beats 'em off.

Imoinda *enters.*

Imo. I'm tost about by my tempestuous Fate,
And no where must have rest; *Indians,* or *English!*

(21)

Whoever has me, I am still a Slave.
No matter whose I am, since I'm no more
My Royal Master's ; since I'm his no more.
O I was happy ! nay, I will be happy
In the dear Thought that I am still his Wife,
Tho' far divided from him.   [*Draws off to a corner of the Stage*

     After a shout, enter the Governor, with Oroonoko, Blanford, Stan-
       more, *and the Planters.*

Gov. Thou glorious Man ! thou something greater sure
Than *Cæsar* ever was ! that single Arm
Has sav'd us all: accept our general thanks.
       All bow to Oroonoko.
And what we can do more to recompence
Such noble Services, you shall command.
Clemene too shall thank you, ——— she is safe———
Look up, and bless your brave deliverer.
     [*Brings* Clemene *forward, looking down on the ground.*
   Oro. Bless me indeed !
   Blan. You start !
   Oro. O all you Gods !
Who govern this great World, and bring about
Things strange and unexpected, can it be ?
   Gov. What is't you stare at so ?
   Oro. Answer me some of yon, you who have power,
And have your Senses free : or are you all
Struck through with wonder too?   [*Looking still fixt on her.*
   Blan. What wou'd you know ?
   Oro. My Soul steals from my Body through my Eyes ;
All that is left of Life, I'll gaze away,
And dye upon the pleasure.
   Gov. This is strange !
   Oro. If you but mock me with her Image here:
If she be not *Imoinda*———   { *She looks upon him, and falls into a*
Ha! she faints !   { *Swoon ; he runs to her.*
Nay, then it must be she ; It is *Imoinda* :
My Heart confesses her, and leaps for joy,
To welcome her to her own Empire here.
I feel her all, in every part of me.
O! let me press her in my eager Arms,
Wake her to life, and with this kindling Kiss
Give back that Soul she only sent to me.   [*Kisses her.*
   Gov. I am amaz'd !
   Blan. I am as much as you.
   Oro. Imoinda ! O ! thy Oroonoko calls.
       [Imoinda *coming to Life.*
   Imo. My Oroonoko ! O ! I can't believe
What any Man can say. But if I am
To be deceiv'd, there's something in that Name,

D 2   That

That Voice, that Face,
O if I know my felf, I cannot be miftaken.   [*Staring on him.*
                                     [*Runs and embraces* Oroonoko.
   Oro. Never here;
You cannot be miftaken. I am yours,
Your *Oroonoko*, all that you wou'd have,
Your tender loving Husband.
   Imo. All indeed
That I wou'd have. My Husband! then I am
Alive, and waking to the Joys I feel;
They were fo great, I cou'd not think 'em true.
But I believe all that you fay to me;
For truth it felf, and everlafting Love
Grows in this Breaft, and pleafure in thefe arms.
   Oro. Take, take me all; enquire into my heart,
(You know the way to every fecret there)
My Heart, the facred treafury of Love:
And if, in abfence, I have mif-employ'd
A Mite from the rich ftore; if I have fpent
A Wifh, a Sigh, but what I fent to you;
May I be curft to wifh, and figh in vain,
And you not pity me.
   Imo. O! I believe,
And know you by my felf. If thefe fad Eyes,
Since laft we parted, have beheld the Face
Of any Comfort; or once wifh'd to fee
The light of any other Heav'n but you;
May I be ftruck this moment blind, and lofe
Your bleffed light, never to find you more.
   Oro. Imoinda! O! this feparation
Has made you dearer, if it can be fo,
Than you were ever to me. You appear
Like a kind Star to my benighted Steps,
To guide me on my way to happinefs.
I cannot mifs it now. Governor, Friend,
You think me mad; but let me blefs you all,
Who any way have been the Inftruments
Of finding her again. Imoinda's found!
And every thing that I wou'd have in her.
                  Embracing her in the moft paffionate fondnefs
   Stan. Where's your Miftrefs now, Governor?
   Gov. Why, where moft mens Miftreffes are forc'd to be fometimes,
With her Husband, it feems; but I won't lofe her fo.   [*Afide.*
   Stan. He has fought luftily for her, and deferves her, I'll fay that for him.
   Blan. Sir, we congratulate your happinefs; I do it heartily.
   Gov. And all of us; but how it comes to pafs ——
   Oro. That will require more precious time than I can fpare you now.
I have a thoufand things to ask of her,
And fhe as many more to know of me.
                                       E.

But you have made me happier, I confefs,
Acknowledge it, much happier, than I
Have words, or pow'r to tell you. Captain, you,
Ev'n you, who moft have wrong'd me, I forgive.
I won't fay you have betray'd me now ;
I'll think you but the minifter of Fate,
To bring me to my lov'd *Imoinda* here.

Imo. How, how fhall I receive you ? how be worthy
Of fuch Endearments, all this tendernefs ?
Thefe are the Tranfports of Profperity,
When Fortune fmiles upon us.

Oro. Let the Fools, who follow Fortune, live upon her fmiles.
All our Profperity is plac'd in Love.
We have enough of that to make us happy.
This little fpot of Earth you ftand upon,
Is more to me, than the extended Plains
Of my great Father's Kingdom. Here I reign
In full delights, in Joys to Pow'r unknown ;
Your Love my Empire, and your Heart my Throne,

ACT III. SCENE I.

[Aboan *with Slaves,* Hottman.]

Hott. WHat ! to be Slaves to Cowards ! Slaves to Rogues !
Who can't defend themfelves !

Abo. Who is this Fellow ? he talks as if he were acquainted
With our defign : Is he one of us ? [*Afide to hi*

Slav. Not yet ; but he will be glad to make one, I believe.

Abo. He makes a mighty noife.

Hott. Go, fneak in Corners, whifper out your Griefs,
For fear your Mafters hear you : cringe and crouch
Under the bloody whip, like beaten Currs,
That lick their Wounds, and know no other cure.
All, wretches all ! you feel their cruelty,
As much as I can feel, but dare not groan.
For my part, while I have a Life and Tongue,
I'll curfe the Authors of my Slavery.

Abo. Have you been long a Slave ?

Hott. Yes, many years.

Abo. And do you only curfe ?

Hott. Curfe ? only curfe ? I cannot conjure
To raife the Spirits of other Men :
I am but one. O ! for a Soul of fire,
To warm, and animate our Common Caufe,
And make a body of us, then I wou'd
Do fomething more than curfe.

Abo. That body set on Foot, you wou'd be one,
A Limb, to lend it motion.

Hat. I wou'd be the Heart of it : the Head, the Hand, and Heart.
Wou'd I cou'd see the day.

Abo. You will do all your self.

Hott. I wou'd do more than I shall speak : but I may find a time.

Abo. The time may come to you ; be ready for't.
Methinks he talks too much : I'll know him more,
Before I trust him farther.

Slav. If he dares half what he says, he'll be of use to us.

[*Enter* Blanford *to 'em.*]

Blan. If there be any one among you here,
That did belong to *Oroonoko,* speak,
I come to him.

Abo. I did belong to him : *Aboan,* my Name.

Blan. You are the Man I want ; pray, come with me. [*Exeunt.*

SCENE II.

[Oroonoko *and* Imoinda.]

Oro. I do not blame my Father for his Love ;
(Tho' that had been enough to ruin me)
'Twas Nature's fault, that made you like the Sun,
The reasonable worship of Mankind ;
He cou'd not help his Adoration.
Age had not lock'd his Senses up so close,
But he had Eyes, that open'd to his Soul,
And took your Beauties in ; he felt your pow'r,
And therefore I forgive his loving you.
But when I think on his Barbarity,
That cou'd expose you to so many Wrongs ;
Driving you out to wretched Slavery,
Only for being mine ; then I confess,
I wish I cou'd forget the Name of Son,
That I might curse the Tyrant.

Imo. I will bless him, for I have found you here ; Heav'n only knows
What is reserv'd for us ; but if we guess
The future by the past, our Fortune must
Be wonderful, above the common size
Of good or ill ; it must be in extreams ;
Extreamly happy, or extreamly wretched.

Oro. 'Tis in our pow'r to make it happy now.

Imo. But not to keep it so. [*Enter* Blanford *and* Aboan.

Blan. My Royal Lord ! I have a Present for you.

Oro. Aboan !

Abo. Your lowest Slave.

Oro. My try'd and valu'd Friend.
This worthy Man always prevents my wants ; I o'ly

I only wifh'd, and he has brought thee to me.
Thou art furpriz'd; carry thy duty there;

[Aboan *goes to* Imoinda,
and falls at her Feet.

While I acknowledge mine, how fhall I thank you?
  Blan. Believe me, honeft to your intereft,
And I am more than paid. I have fecur'd,
That all your Followers fhall be gently us'd.
This Gentleman, your chiefeft Favourite,
Shall wait upon your Perfon, while you ftay among us.
  Oro. I owe every thing to you.
  Blan. You muft not think you are in Slavery.
  Oro. I do not find I am.
  Blan. Kind Heaven has miraculoufly fent
Thofe Comforts, that may teach you to expect
Its farther care, in your deliverance.
  Oro. I fometimes think my felf, Heaven is concern'd
For my deliverance.
  Blan. It will be foon;
You may expect it. Pray, in the mean time,
Appear as cheerful as you can among us.
You have fome Enemies, that reprefent
You dangerous, and wou'd be glad to find
A Reafon, in your difcontent, to fear;
They watch your looks. But they are honeft Men,
Who are your Friends, you are fecure in them.
  Oro. I thank you for your caution.
  Blan. I will leave you;
And be affur'd I wifh you liberty.   *Exit.*
  Abo. He fpeaks you very fair.
  Oro. He means me fair.
  Abo. If he fhould not, my Lord.
  Oro. If, he fhould not.
I'll not fufpect his Truth; but if I did,
What fhall I get by doubting?
  *Abo.*You fecure,not to be difappointed; but befides,
There's this advantage in fufpecting him;
When you put off the hopes of other men,
You will rely upon your God-like felf;
And then you may be fure of liberty.
  Oro. Be fure of liberty! what doft thou mean;
Advifing to rely upon my felf?
I think I may be fure on't, we muft wait;
  'Tis worth a little patience.
  Abo. O my Lord!
  Oro. What doft thou drive at?
  Abo. Sir, another time,
You wou'd have found it fooner: but I fee
Love has your Heart, and takes up all your Thoughts.
  Oro. And canft thou blame me?

[*Turning to* Imoinda.

Abo.

Abo. Sir, I muſt not blame you.
But as your fortune ſtands there is a Paſſion
(Your Pardon Royal Miſtreſs, I muſt ſpeak :)
That wou'd become you better than your Love:
A brave reſentment ; which inſpir'd by you,
Might kindle, and diffuſe a generous rage
Among the Slaves, to rouze and ſhake our Chains,
And ſtruggle to be free.

   Oro. How can we help our ſelves ?

   Abo. I knew you, when you wou'd have found a way.
How, help our ſelves ! the very *Indians* teach us ;
We need but to attempt our Liberty,
And we may carry it. We have Hands ſufficient,
Double the number of our Maſter's force,
Ready to be employ'd. What hinders us
To ſet 'em then at work ? we want but you,
To head our enterprize, and bid us ſtrike.

   Oro. What wou'd you do ?

   Abo. Cut your Oppreſſors Throats.

   Oro. And you wou'd have me joyn in your deſign of Murder ?

   Abo. It deſerves a better Name ;
But be it what it will, 'tis juſtified
By ſelf-defence, and natural liberty.

   Oro. I'll hear no more on't.

   Abo. I am ſorry for't.

   Oro. Nor ſhall you think of it.

   Abo. Not think of it !

   Oro. No, I command you not.

   Abo. Remember, Sir,
You are a Slave your ſelf, and to command,
Is now another's right. Not think of it !
Since the firſt moment they put on my Chains,
I've thought of nothing but the weight of 'em,
And how to throw 'em off ; Can yours ſit eaſy ?

   Oro. I have a ſenſe of my condition,
As painful and as quick as yours can be.
I feel for my *Imoinda* and my ſelf ;
Imoinda, much the tendereſt part of me.
But though I languiſh for my liberty,
I wou'd not buy it at the Chriſtian Price
Of black Ingratitude ; they ſhannot ſay,
That we deſerv'd our Fortune by our Crimes.
Murder the innocent !

   Abo. The innocent !

   Oro. Theſe men are ſo, whom you wou'd riſe againſt.
If we are Slaves, they did not make us Slaves ;
But bought us in an honeſt way of Trade,
As we have done before 'em, bought and ſold

Many a wretch, and never thought it wrong.
They paid our Price for us, and we are now
Their Property, a part of their Estate,
To manage as they please. Mistake me not,
I do not tamely say, that we should bear
All they could lay upon us; but we find,
The load so light, so little to be felt,
(Considering they have us in their power,
And may inflict what grievances they please)
We ought not to complain.

Abo. My Royal Lord!
You do not know the heavy Grievances,
The Toyls, the Labours, weary Drudgeries,
Which they impose; Burdens more fit for Beasts,
For senseless Beasts to bear, than thinking Men.
Then if you saw the bloody Cruelties
They execute on every slight Offence;
Nay, sometimes in their proud, insulting sport:
How worse than Dogs they lash their Fellow-Creatures;
Your heart wou'd bleed for 'em. O cou'd you know
How many Wretches lift their Hands and Eyes
To you, for their Relief.

Oro. I pity 'em,
And wish I cou'd with honesty do more.

Abo. You must do more, and may with honesty.
O Royal Sir, remember who you are,
A Prince, born for the good of other Men;
Whose Godlike Office is to draw the Sword
Against Oppression, and set free Mankind;
And this, I'm sure, you think Oppression now.
What though you have not felt these miseries,
Never believe you are oblig'd to them;
They have their selfish reasons, may be, now,
For using of you well; but there will come
A time when you must have your share of 'em.

Oro. You see how little cause I have to think so;
Favour'd in my own Person, in my Friends;
Indulg'd in all that can concern my care,
In my *Imoinda's* soft Society.

Abo. And therefore would you lie contented down,
In the forgetfulness and arms of Love,
To get young Princes for 'em?

Oro. Say'st thou! ha!

Abo. Princes, the Heirs of Empire, and the last
Of your illustrious Lineage, to be born
To pamper up their Pride, and be their Slaves?

Oro. Imoinda! save me, save me from that thought.

Imo. There is no safety from it; I have long
Suffer'd it with a Mother's labouring pains;

E

And can no longer. Kill me, kill me now,
While I am bleſt, and happy in your Love ;
Rather than let me live to ſee you hate me ;
As you muſt hate me ; me, the only Cauſe,
The Fountain of theſe flowing miſeries :
Dry up this Spring of Life, this pois'nous Spring,
That ſwells ſo faſt, to overwhelm us all.

Oro. Shall the dear Babe, the eldeſt of my hopes,
Whom I begot a Prince, be born a Slave ?
The Treaſure of this Temple was deſign'd
T' enrich a Kingdom's Fortune ; ſhall it here
Be ſeiz'd upon by vile unhallow'd hands,
To be employ'd in uſes moſt prophane?

Abo. In moſt unworthy uſes ; think of that ;
And while you may, prevent it. O my Lord !
Rely on nothing that they ſay to you.
They ſpeak you fair, I know, and bid you wait.
But think what 'tis to wait on promiſes ;
And promiſes of Men who know no tye
Upon their Words, againſt their intereſt ;
And where's their intereſt in freeing you ?

Imo. O ! where indeed, to loſe ſo many Slaves ?

Abo. Nay grant this man you think ſo much your friend,
Be honeſt, and intends all that he ſays ;
He is but one ; and in a Government,
Where, he confeſſes, you have Enemies,
That watch your looks ; what looks can you put on,
To pleaſe theſe men, who are before reſolv'd
To read 'em their own way ? Alas, my Lord !
If they incline to think you dangerous,
They have their knaviſh Arts to make you ſo.
And then who knows how far their cruelty
May carry their revenge?

Imo. To every thing
That does belong to you ; your Friends, and me ;
I ſhall be torn from you, forc'd away,
Helpleſs, and miſerable : ſhall I live
To ſee that day agen?

Oro. That day ſhall never come.

Abo. I know you are perſuaded to believe
The Governor's arrival will prevent
Theſe miſchiefs, and beſtow your liberty ;
But who is ſure of that ? I rather fear
More miſchiefs from his coming ; he is young,
Luxurious, paſſionate, and amorous.
Such a Complexion, and made bold by Power,
To countenance all he is prone to do ;
Will know no bounds, no Law againſt his Luſts ;

If, in a fit of his Intemperance,
With a strong hand he should resolve to seize,
And force my Royal Miftrefs from your Arms,
How can you help your felf?

   Oro. Ha! thou haft rouz'd
The Lion in his den, he ftalks abroad,
And the wide Foreft trembles at his roar.
I find the danger now; my Spirits ftart
At the alarm, and from all quarters come
To Man my Heart, the Citadel of Love.
Is there a Power on Earth to force you from me?
And fhall I not refift it? not ftrike firft,
To keep, to fave you? to prevent that Curfe?
This is your Caufe, and fhall it not prevail?
O! you were born all ways to conquer me.
Now I am fafhion'd to thy purpofe; fpeak,
What Combination, what Confpiracy,
Wou'dft thou engage me in? I'll undertake
All thou wou'dft have me now for liberty,
For the great Caufe of Love and Liberty.

   Abo. Now, my great Mafter, you appear your felf.
And fince we have you join'd in our defign,
It cannot fail us. I have mufter'd up
The choiceft Slaves, Men who are fenfible
Of their condition, and feem moft refolv'd;
They have their feveral Parties.

   Oro. Summon 'em,
Affemble 'em; I will come forth, and fhew
My felf among 'em; if they are refolv'd,
I'll lead their formoft refolutions.

   Abo. I have provided thofe will follow you.

   Oro. With this referve in our proceeding ftill,
The means that lead us to our liberty
Muft not be bloody.

   Abo. You command in all.
We fhall expect you, Sir.

   Oro. You fhannot long.

    Exeunt Oroonoko *and* Imoinda *at one Door,* Aboan *at another.*

SCENE III.

[Welldon *coming in before Mrs.* Lackitt.]

   Wid. Thefe unmannerly *Indians* were fomething unfeafonable, to difturb us juft in the nick, Mr. *Welldon*; but I have the Parfon within call ftill, to do us the good turn.

   Wel. We had beft ftay a little I think, to fee things fettled again, had not we? Marriage is a ferious thing, you know.

   Wid. What do you talk of a ferious thing, Mr. *Welldon?* I think you have found me fufficiently ferious; I have marri'd my Son to your Sifter, to pleafure you;

you ; and now I come to claim your promise to me, you tell me Marriage is a serious thing.

Well. Why, is it not ?

Wid. Fiddle faddle, I know what it is ; 'tis not the first time I have been marry'd, I hope ; but I shall begin to think you don't design to do fairly by me, so I shall.

Well. Why indeed, Mrs. *Lackitt*, I am afraid I can't do as fairly as I wou'd by you. 'Tis what you must know, first or last ; and I shou'd be the worst man in the world to conceal it any longer ; therefore I must own to you, that I am marri'd already.

Wid. Marry'd ! you don't say so I hope ! how have you the Conscience to tell me such a thing to my face ! have you abus'd me then, fool'd and cheated me ? What do you take me for, Mr. *Welldon* ? do you think I am to be serv'd at this rate ? but you shan't find me the silly creature you think me ; I wou'd have you to know I understand better things, than to ruin my Son without a valuable consideration. If I can't have you, I can keep my Money. Your Sister shan't have the catch of him she expected. I won't part with a Shilling to 'em.

Well. You made the match your self, you know, you can't blame me.

Wid. Yes, yes, I can, and do blame you ;
You might have told me before you were marry'd.

Well. I wou'd not have told you now ; but you follow'd me so close, I was forc'd to't : Indeed I am marry'd in *England* ; but 'tis as if I were not, for I have been parted from my Wife a great while ; and to do reason on both sides, we hate one another heartily. Now I did design, and will marry you still, if you ll have a little patience.

Wid. A likely business truly.

Well. I have a Friend in *England* that I will write to, to poyson my Wife, and then I can marry you with a good Conscience : If you love me as you say you do, you'll consent to that, I'm sure.

Wid. And will he do it, do you think ?

Well. At the first word, or he is not the Man I take him to be.

Wid. Well, you are a dear Devil, Mr. *Welldon* :
And wou'd you poyson your Wife for me ?

Well. I wou'd do any thing for you.

Wid. Well, I am mightily oblig'd to you.
But 'twill be a great while before you can have an answer of your Letter.

Well. 'Twill be a great while indeed.

Wid. In the mean time, Mr. *Welldon*———

Well. Why in the mean time———
Here's company ; we'll settle that within.
I'll follow you.   [*Exit Widow.*

[*Enter Stanmore.*]

Stan. So, Sir, you carry your business swimmingly ;
You have stollen a Wedding, I hear.

Well. Ay, my Sister is marri'd, and I am very near being run away with my self.

Stan. The Widow will have you then.

Well.

Well. You come very feasonably to my refcue:
Jack Stanmore is to be had, I hope.
   Stan. At half an hours warning.
   Well. I muft advife with you.   [*Exeunt.*

SCENE IV.

[Oroonoko *with* Aboan, Hottman, *Slaves.*]

   Oro. Impoffible! nothing's impoffible :
We know our ftrength only by being tri'd:
If you objeét the Mountains, Rivers, Woods
Unpaffable, that lye before our March.
Woods we can fet on fire: we fwim by Nature :
What can oppofe us then, but we may tame?
All things fubmit to virtuous induftry :
That we can carry with us, that is ours.
   Slave. Great Sir, we have attended all you faid,
With filent joy and admiration :
And were we only Men, wou'd follow fuch,
So great a Leader, thro' the untri'd World.
But oh! confider we have other Names,
Husbands and Fathers, and have things more dear
To us than Life, our Children and our Wives,
Unfit for fuch an Expedition ;
What muft become of them?
   Oro. We wonnot wrong
The virtue of our Women, to believe
There is a Wife among 'em would refufe
To fhare her Husband's fortune. What is hard,
We muft make eafy to 'em in our Love, while we live,
And have our Limbs, we can take care for them ;
Therefore I ftill propofe to lead our march
Down to the Sea, and plant a Colony ;
Where, in our native innocence, we fhall live
Free, and be able to defend our felves ;
Till ftrefs of weather, or fome accident
Provide a Ship for us.
   Abo. An accident! the luckieft accident prefents it felf:
The very Ship that brought and made us Slaves,
Swims in the River ftill : I fee no caufe
But we may feize on that.
   Oro. It fhall be fo :
There is a juftice in it pleafes me.
Do you agree to it ?   [*To the Slaves.*
   Omn. We follow you.
   Oro. You do not relifh it.   [*To* Hottman.
   Hott. I am afraid
You'll find it difficult and dangerous.
   Abo. Are you the Man to find the danger firft ?
You fhou'd have giv'n example. Dangerous!   I thought

I thought you had not underſtood the word ;
You, who wou'd be the Head, the Hand, and Heart ;
Sir, I remember you, you can talk well ;
I wonnot doubt but you'll maintain your word.

   Oro. This Fellow is not right, I'll try him further.   [*To Aboan.*
The danger will be certain to us all ;
And Death moſt certain in miſcarrying.
We muſt expect no mercy, if we fail :
Therefore our way muſt be not to expect ;
We'll put it out of expectation,
By Death upon the place, or Liberty.
There is no mean but Death or Liberty.
There's no Man here, I hope, but comes prepar'd
For all that can befall him.

   Abo. Death is all ;
In moſt conditions of humanity
To be deſir'd, but to be ſhunn'd in none :
The remedy of many, wiſh of ſome,
And certain end of all.
If there be one among us, who can fear
The face of Death appearing like a Friend,
As in this cauſe of Honour Death muſt be ;
How will he tremble, when he ſees him dreſt
In the wild fury of our Enemies :
In all the terrors of their cruelty ?
For now if we ſhou'd fall into their hands,
Cou'd they invent a thouſand murd'ring ways :
By racking Torments we ſhou'd feel 'em all.

   Hott. What will become of us ?
   Oro. Obſerve him now.   [*To Aboan concerning Hottman.*
I cou'd die altogether, like a Man,
As you, and you, and all of us may do,
But who can promiſe for his bravery
Upon the Rack? where fainting, weary life,
Hunted thro' every Limb, is forc'd to feel
An agonizing death of all its parts ?
Who can bear this ? reſolve to be impal'd ?
His Skin flead off, and roaſted yet alive ?
The quivering fleſh torn from his broken Bones,
By burning Pincers? who can bear theſe Pains?

   Hott. They are not to be born.   [*Diſcovering all the confuſion of fear.*
   Oro. You ſee him now, this Man of mighty words !
   Abo. How his Eyes roul !
   Oro. He cannot hide his fear :
I try'd him this way, and have found him out.
   Abo. I cou'd not have believ'd it. Such a Blaze,
And not a ſpark of Fire !
   Oro. His violence
Made me ſuſpect him firſt ; now I'm convinc'd.

                                             Abo.

Abo. What shall we do with him?

Oro. He is not fit——

Abo. Fit! hang him, he is only fit to be
Just what he is, to live and dye a Slave,
The base Companion of his servile Fears.

Oro. We are not safe with him.

Abo. Do you think so?

Oro. He'll certainly betray us.

Abo. That he shan't,
I can take care of that. I have a way
To take him off his evidence.

Oro. What way?

Abo. I'll stop his mouth before you, stab him here,
And then let him inform. [*Going to stab* Hottman, Oroonoko *holds him.*

Oro. Thou art not mad?

Abo. I wou'd secure our selves.

Oro. It shannot be this way; nay cannot be;
His Murder wou'd alarm all the rest,
Make 'em suspect us of Barbarity,
And, may be, fall away from our design.
We'll not set out in Blood: we have, my Friends,
This Night to furnish what we can provide
For our security and just defence.
If there be one among us we suspect
Of baseness or vile fear, it will become
Our common care to have our Eyes on him:
I wonnot name the Man.

Abo. You guess at him. [*To* Hottman.

Oro. To morrow, early as the breaking day,
We rendezvous behind the Citron Grove.
That Ship secur'd, we may transport our selves
To our respective homes, my Father's Kingdom
Shall open her wide arms to take you in,
And nurse you for her own, adopt you all,
All who will follow me.

Omn. All, all follow you.

Oro. There I can give you all your liberty,
Bestow its Blessings, and secure 'em yours.
There you shall live with honour, as becomes
My Fellow-sufferers, and worthy Friends::
This if we do succeed: But if we fall
In our attempt, 'tis nobler still to dye,
Than drag the galling yoke of slavery. [*Exeunt omnes.*

ACT IV. SCENE I.

[Welldon *and* Jack Stanmore.]

Well. You see, honest *Jack,* I have been industrious for you: you must take
some pains now to serve your self.

J. Stan.

J. Stan. Gad, Mr. *Welldon,* I have taken a great deal of pains : And if the Widow speaks honestly, faith and troth, She'll tell you what a pains-taker I am.

Well. Fie, fie, not me : I am her Husband you know ;
She won't tell me what pains you have taken with her :
Besides, she takes you for me.

J. Stan. That's true : I forgot you had marry'd her,
But if you knew all ——

Well. 'Tis no matter for my knowing all : if she does ——

J. Stan. Ay, ay, she does know, and more than ever she knew since she was a woman, for the time, I will be bold to say ; for I have done ——

Well. The Devil take you, you'll never have done.

J Stan. As old as she is, she has a wrinckle behind more than she had, I believe ——
For I have taught her what she never knew in her life before.

Well. What care I what wrinckles she has? or what you have taught her? If you'll let me advise you, you may; if not, you may prate on, and ruin the whole design.

J. Stan. Well, well, I have done.

VVell. No body but your Cousin and you and I know any thing of this matter. I have marry'd Mrs. *Lackitt,* and put you to bed to her, which she knows nothing of, to serve you: in two or three days I'll bring it about so, to resign up my claim, with her consent, quietly to you.

J. Stan. But how will you do it ?

VVell. That must be my business; in the mean time, if you should make any noise, 'twill come to her Ears, and be impossible to reconcile her.

J. Stan. Nay, as for that, I know the way to reconcile her, I warrant you.

VVell. But how will you get her Money ? I am marry'd to her,

J. Stan. That I don't know indeed.

VVell. You must leave it to me, you find; all the pains I shall put you to will be to be silent : you can hold your Tongue for two or three days?

J. Stan. Truly, not well, in a matter of this nature : I should be very unwilling to lose the reputation of this nights work, and the pleasure of telling.

VVell. You must mortify that vanity a little : you will have time enough to brag, and lie of your Manhood, when you have her in a bare-fac'd condition to disprove you.

J. Stan. Well, I'll try what I can do: the hopes of her Money must do it.

VVell. You'll come at night again ? 'tis your own business.

J. Stan. But you have the credit on't.

VVell. 'Twill be your own another day, as the Widow says.
Send your Cousin to me: I want his advice.

J. Stan. I want to be recruited, I'm sure, a good Breakfast, and to Bed: She has rock'd my Cradle sufficiently. [*Exit.*

VVell. She would have a Husband ; and if all be as he says, she has no reason to complain: But there's no relying on what the Men say upon these occasions: they have the benefit of their bragging, by recommending their abilities to other Women: theirs is a trading Estate, that lives upon credit, and increases by removing it out of one Bank into another. Now poor Women have not these opportunities ; we must keep our Stocks dead by us at home, to be ready for a purchase when it comes, a Husband, let him be never so dear, and be glad of him : or venture our Fortunes abroad on such rotten security, that the Principal and Interest, nay very often our Persons are in danger. If the Women wou'd agree (which they never will) to call home their Effects, how many proper Gentlemen wou'd sneak into another way of living, for want of being responsible in this? then Husbands wou'd be cheaper. Here comes the Widow, she'll tell truth: she'll not bear false Witness against her own interest, I know.

[*Enter Widow* Lackitt.]

Well. Now, Mrs. *Lackit.*

Wid. Well, well, *Lackit,* or what you will now ; now I am marry'd to you ; I am very well pleas'd with what I have done, I assure you.

Well. And with what I have done too, I hope.

Wid. Ah *! Mr. Welldon !* I say nothing, but you're a dear Man, and I did not think it had been in you.

Well. I have more in me than you imagine.

Wid. No, no, you can't have more than I imagine ; 'tis impossible to have more ; you have enough for any Woman, in an honest way, that I will say for you.

Well. Then I find you are satisfied.

Wid. Satisfied ! no indeed ; I'm not to be satisfied with you or without you ; to be satisfied, is to have enough of you ; now 'tis a folly to lye, I shall never think I can have enough of you. I shall be very fond of you : would you have me fond of you? What do you do to me, to make me love you so well ?

Well. Can't you tell what ?

Wid. Go, there's no speaking to you ; you bring all the Blood of one's Body into one's face, so you do ; why do you talk so ?

Well. Why, how do I talk ?

Wid. You know how ; but a little colour becomes me, I believe ; how do I look to day ?

Well. O *!* most lovingly, most amiably.

Wid. Nay, this can't be long a secret, I find, I shall discover it by my Countenance.

Well. The Women will find you out, you look so cheerfully.

Wid. But do I, do I really look so cheerfully, so amiably ? there's no such Paint in the World as the natural glowing of a Complexion. Let 'em find me out, if they please, poor Creatures, I pity 'em ; they envy me, I'm sure, and would be glad to mend their looks upon the same occasion. The young jillflirting Girls, forsooth, believe no body must have a Husband, but themselves ; but I would have 'em to know there are other things to be taken care of, besides their Green-Sickness.

Well. Ay, sure, or the Physicians wou'd have but little practice.

Wid. Mr. *Welldon,* what must I call you ; I must have some pretty fond name or other for you ; what shall I call you ?

Well. I thought you lik'd my own name.

Wid. Yes, yes, I like it, but I must have a nickname for you ; most Women have nicknames for their Husbands ——————

Well. Cuckold.   F   *Wid.*

Wid. No, no, but 'tis very pretty before Company; It looks negligent, and is the fashion, you know.

Well. To be negligent of their Husbands, it is indeed.

Wid. Nay then, I won't be in the fashion; for I can never be negligent of dear Mr. *Welldon*; and to convince you, here's something to encourage you not to be negligent of me.   *Gives him a Purse and a little Casket.*
Five hundred pounds in Gold in this; and Jewels to the value of Five hundr.d pounds more in this.   [*Welldon opens the Casket.*

Well. Ay, marry, this will encourage me indeed.

Wid. There are comforts in marrying an elderly Woman, Mr. *Welldon.* Now a young Woman wou'd have fanci'd she had paid you with her person, or had done you the favour.

Well. What do you talk of young Women? you are as young as any of 'em, in every thing but their folly and ignorance.

Wid. And do you think me so? but I have no reason to suspect you. Was not I seen at your house this Morning, do you think?

Well. You may venture again; you'll come at night, I suppose.

Wid. O dear! at night? so soon?

Well. Nay, if you think it so soon.

Wid. O! no, it is not for that, Mr. *Welldon*, but ———

Well. You won't come then.

Wid. Won't! I don't say I wont; that is not a word for a Wife; If you command me ———

Well. To please your self.

Wid. I will come to please you.

Well. To please your self, own it.

Wid. Well, well, to please my self then, you're the strangest Man in the World, nothing can 'scape you; you'll to the bottom of every thing.
[*Enter* Daniel, Lucia *following.*]

Dan. What wou'd you have? what do you follow me for?

Luc. Why, mayn't I follow you? I must follow you now all the world over.

Dan. Hold you, hold you there; not so far by a mile or two; I have enough of your Company already by'r-lady; and something to spare; you may go home to your Brother, an' you will, I have no farther to do with you.

Wid. Why, *Daniel,* Child, thou art not out of thy wits sure, art thou?

Dan. Nay, marry, I don't know; but I am very near it, I believe; I am alter'd for the worse mightily since you saw me; And she has been the cause of it there.

Wid. How so, Child?

Dan. I told you before what would come on't, of putting me to bed to strange Woman; but you wou'd not be said nay.

Wid. She is your Wife now, Child, you must love her.

Dan. Why, so I did at first.

Wid. But you must love her always.

Dan. Always! I lov'd her as long as I cou'd, Mother, and as long as love was good, I believe, for I find now I don't care a fig for her.

Luc. Why, you lubberly, slovenly, misbegotten Blockhead.———

Wid. Nay, Mistress *Lucy*, say any thing else, and spare not; but as to
begettin

begetting, that touches me, he is as honestly begotten, though I say it, that he is the worse agen.

Luc. I see all good nature is thrown away upon you——

Wid. It was so with his Father before him; he takes after him.

Luc. And therefore I will use you as you deserve, you Tony.

VVid. Indeed he deserves bad enough; but don't call him out of his name, his name is *Daniel*, you know.

Dan. She may call me Hermophrodite, if she will,
For I hardly know whether I'm a Boy or a Girl.

VVell. A Boy, I warrant thee, as long as thou liv'st.

Dan. Let her call me what she pleases, Mother,
Tis not her Tongue that I'm afraid of.

Luc. I will make such a Beast of thee, such a Cuckold!

Wid. O pray, no, I hope; do nothing rashly, Mrs. *Lucy.*

Luc. Such a Cuckold will I make of thee!

Dan. I had rather be a Cuckold, than what you wou'd make of me in a week, I'm sure; I have no more manhood left in me already, than there is, saving the mark, in one of my Mother's old under Petticoats here.

VVid. Sirrah, Sirrah, meddle with your Wife's Petticoats, and let your Mother's alone, you ungracious Bird, you.   [*Beats him.*

Dan. Why, is the Devil in the Woman? what have I said now? Do you know, if you were ask'd, I trow? but you are all of a bundle; ev'n hang together; he that unties you, makes a Rod for his own Tail; and so he will find it, that has any thing to do with you.

VVid. Ay, Rogue enough, you shall find it; I have a Rod for your Tail still.

Dan. No Wife, and I care not.

Wid. I'll swinge you into better manners, you Booby. [*Beats him off,* Exit.

VVell. You have consummated our Project upon him.

Luc. Nay, if I have a Limb of the Fortune,
care not who has the whole Body of the Fool.

VVell. That you shall, and a large one, I promise you.

Luc. Have you heard the news? they talk of an *English* Ship in the River.

VVell. I have heard on't, and am preparing to receive it as fast as I can.

Luc. There's something the matter too with the Slaves,
some disturbance or other; I don't know what 'tis.

VVell. So much the better still;
Fish in troubled Waters:
We shall have fewer Eyes upon us.
nay, go you home, and be ready to assist me in your part of the design.

Luc. I can't fail in mine.   [*Exit.*

VVell. The Widow has furnish'd me, I thank her, to carry it on.
now I have got a Wife, 'tis high time to think of getting a Husband.
carry my Fortune about me:
Thousand Pounds in Gold and Jewels.
let me see ——
will be a considerable Trust;
and I think I shall lay it out to advantage.

F 2   [*Enter*

[*Enter Stanmore.*]

Stan. So *Welldon, Jack* has told me his fucccſs, and his hopes of marry-ing the Widow by your means.

Well. I have ſtrain'd a point, *Stanmore,* upon your account, to be ſerviceable to your Family.

Stan. I take it upon my account, and am very much oblig'd to you. But here we are all in an Uproar.

Well. So they ſay ; What's the matter ?

Stan. A Mutiny among the Slaves ; *Oroonoko* is at the head of 'em, Our Governor is gone out with his Raſcally Militia againſt 'em, What it may come to no body knows.

Well. For my part, I ſhall do as well as the reſt ; but I'm concern'd for my Siſter, and Couſin, whom I expect in the Ship from *England.*

Stan There's no danger of 'em.

Well. I have a Thouſand Pounds here in Gold and Jewels, for my Couſins uſe, that I wou'd more particularly take care of ; 'tis too great a Sum to ven-ture at home ; and I wou'd not have her wrong'd of it ; therefore, to ſecure it, I think my beſt way will be, to put it into your keeping.

Stan. You have a very good opinion of my honeſty. [*Takes the Purſe and Caſke.*

Well. I have indeed ; if any thing ſhould happen to me, in this buſtle, as no body is ſecure of accidents, I know you will take my Couſin into your protection and care.

Stan. You may be ſure on't.

Well. If you hear ſhe is dead, as ſhe may be, then I deſire you to accept of the Thouſand Pound, as a Legacy, and Token of my Friendſhip ; my Si-ſter is provided for.

Stan. Why, you amaze me : but you are never the nearer dying, I hope, for making your Will ?

Well. Not a jot ; but I love to be beforehand with Fortune, If ſhe comes ſafe, this is not a place for a ſingle Woman, you know ; Pray ſee her married as ſoon as you can.

Stan. If ſhe be as handſome as her Picture, I can promiſe her a Husband.

Well. If you like her, when you ſee her, I wiſh nothing ſo much as have you marry her your ſelf.

Stan. From what I have heard of her, and my Engagements to you, muſt be her Fault, if I don't : I hope to have her from your own Hand.

Well. And I hope to give her to you, for all this.

Stan. Ay, ay, hang theſe melancholy Reflections. Your Generoſity has engag'd all my Services.

Well. I always thought you worth making a Friend.

Stan. You ſhan't find your good Opinion thrown away upon me ; I in your debt, and ſhall think ſo long as I live. [*Ex*

S C E N E II.

Enter on one ſide of the Stage Oroonoko, Aboan, *with the Slaves,* Imoinda *with a and Q. iver, the VVomen, ſome leading, others carrying their Children upon their b*

Oro. The Women, with their Children, fall behind.

Imti

Imoinda you muft not expofe your felf ;
Retire, my Love ; I almoft feat for you.

  Imo. I fear no Danger ; Life or Death I will enjoy with you.

  Oro. My Perfon is your Guard.

  Abo. Now, Sir, blame your felf; if you had not prevented my cutting his Throat, that Coward there had not difcover'd us ; He comes now to up-braid you.

      Enter on the other fide Governor, talking to Hottman, *with his Rabble.*

  Gov. This is the very thing I wou'd have wifht.

Your honeft Service to the Government   [*To* Hottman.
Shall be rewarded with your Liberty.

  Abo. His honeft Service ! call it what it is,
His Villany, the Service of his Fear :
If he pretends to honeft Services,
Let him ftand out, and meet me like a Man.   [*Advancing.*

  Oro. Hold, you ; And you who come againft us, hold ;
I charge you in a general good to all,
And wifh I cou'd command you, to prevent
The bloody Havock of the murdering Sword.
I wou'd not urge Deftruction uncompell'd ;
But if you follow Fate, you find it here.
The Bounds are fet, the Limits of our Lives ;
Between us lies the gaping Gulph of Death,
To fwallow all ; who firft advances——   [*Enter the Capt. with his Crew.*

  Capt. Here, here, here they are, Governor ;
What ! feize upon my Ship !
Come, Boys, fall on——   [*Advancing firft,* Oroonoko *kills him.*

  Oro. Thou art fall'n indeed. Thy own Blood be upon thee.

  Gov. Reft it there ; he did deferve his Death.
Take him away.   [*the Body remov'd.*
You fee, Sir, you and thofe miftaken Men
Muft be our Witneffes we do not come
As Enemies, and thirfting for your Blood.
If we defir'd your Ruin, the Revenge
Of our Companions Death had pufh'd it on.
But that we over-look, in a Regard
To common Safety, and the publick Good.

  Oro. Regard that publick good ; draw off your Men,
And leave us to our Fortune ; We're refolv'd.

  Gov. Refolv'd, on what ? your Refolutions
Are broken, overturn'd, prevented, loft.
What Fortune now can you raife out of 'em ?
Nay, grant we fhou'd draw off, what can you do ?
Where can you move ? What more can you refolve ?
Unlefs it be to throw your felves away.
Famine muft eat you up, if you go on.
You fee, our Numbers cou'd with Eafe compel
What we requeft ; and what do we requeft ?

                             Only

Only to save your selves ?

[*The Women with their Children gathering about the Men.*

Oro. I'll hear no more.

VVomen. Hear him, hear him. He takes no care of us.

Gov. To those poor wretches who have been seduc'd,
And led away, to all and every one,
We offer a full Pardon——

Oro. Then fall on.   [*Preparing to Engage.*

Gov. Lay hold upon't, before it be too late,
Pardon and Mercy.   [*The Women clinging about the Men, they leave* Oroonoko,
and fall upon their Faces, crying out for Pardon.

Slaves. Pardon, Mercy, Pardon.

Oro. Let 'em go all ; now, Governor, I see,
I own the Folly of my Enterprise,
The Rashness of this Action, and must blush
Quite through this Vail of Night, a whitely Shame,
To think I cou'd design to make those free,
Who were by Nature Slaves ; Wretches design'd
To be their Masters Dogs, and lick their Feet.
Whip, whip 'em to the Knowledge of your Gods,
Your Christian Gods, who suffer you to be
Unjust, dishonest, cowardly, and base,
And give 'em your Excuse for being so.
I wou'd not live on the same Earth with Creatures
That only have the Faces of their Kind ;
Why shou'd they look like Men, who are not so ?
When they put off their Noble Natures, for
The groveling qualities of down-cast Beasts,
I wish they had their Tails.

Abo. Then we shou'd know 'em.

Oro. We were too few before for Victory;
We're still enow to dye.   [*To* Imoinda, Aboan.

Blanford *Enters.*

Gov. Live, Royal Sir ;
Live, and be happy long on your own Terms,
Only consent to yield, and you shall have
What Terms you can propose, for you, and yours.

Oro. Consent to yield ! Shall I betray my self ?

Gov. Alas ! we cannot fear, that your small Force,
The Force of two, with a weak Woman's Arm,
Shou'd Conquer us. I speak in the regard
And Honour of your Worth, in my desire
And forwardness to serve so great a Man.
I wou'd not have it lie upon my Thoughts,
That I was the occasion of the fall
Of such a Prince, whose Courage carried on
In a more Noble Cause, wou'd well deserve
The Empire of the World.

Oro. You can speak fair.

Gov. Your Undertaking, tho' it wou'd have brought
So great a loss to us, we must all say
Was generous, and noble ; and shall be
Regarded only as the Fire of Youth,
That will break out sometimes in Gallant.; So
We'll think it but the Natural Impulse,
A rash Impatience of Liberty :
No otherwise.

   Oro. Think it what you will.
I was not born to render an Account
Of what I do, to any but my self.   [*Blanford* *comes forward.*

   Blan. I'm glad you have proceeded by fair means.   [*To the Governor.*
I came to be a Mediator.

   Gov. Try what you can work upon him.

   Oro. Are you come against me too ?

   Blan. Is this to come against you ?   [*Offering his Sword to* Oroonoko.
Unarm'd to put my self into your Hands ?
I come, I hope, to serve you.

   Oro. You have serv'd me ;
I thank you for't ; And I am pleas'd to think
You were my Friend, while I had need of one;
But now 'tis past; this farewel; and be gone.   [*Embraces him.*

   Blan. It is not past, and I must serve you still.
I wou'd make up these Breaches, which the Sword
Will widen more ; and close us all in Love.

   Oro. I know what I have done, and I shou'd be
A Child to think they ever can Forgive ;
Forgive ! were there but that, I wou'd not live
To be Forgiven ; Is there a Power on Earth,
That I can ever need forgiveness from ?

   Blan. You sha' not need it.

   Oro. No, I wonnot need it.

   Blan. You see he offers you your own Conditions,
For you, and yours,

   Oro. I must Capitulate ?
Precariously Compound, on stinted Terms,
To save my Life ?

   Blan. Sir, he imposes none.
You make 'em for your own Security.
If your great Heart cannot descend to treat,
In adverse Fortune, with an Enemy ;
Yet sure, your Honour's safe, you may accept
Offers of Peace, and Safety from a Friend.

   Gov. He will rely on what you say to him ;   [*To* Blanford.
Offer him what you can, I will confirm,
And make all good; Be you my Pledge of Trust.

   Blan. I'll answer with my Life for all he says.

   Gov. Ay, do, and pay the Forfeit if you please.   [*Aside.*
                                       Blan.

Blan. Confider, Sir, can you confent to throw
That Bleffing from you, you fo hardly found,   [*Of* Imoinda.
And fo much valu'd once ?

    Oro. Imoinda ! Oh !
'Tis She that holds me on this Argument
Of tedious Life ; I cou'd refolve it foon,
Were this curft Being only in Debate.
But my *Imoinda* ftruggles in my Soul ;
She makes a Coward of me ; I confefs
I am afraid to part with Her in Death ;
And more afraid of Life to lofe Her here.

    Blan. This way you muft lofe her, think upon
The weaknefs of her Sex, made yet more weak
With her Condition, requiring Reft,
And foft indulging Eafe, to nurfe your Hopes,
And make you a glad Father.

    Oro. There I feel a Father's Fondnefs, and a Husband's Love.
They feize upon my Heart, ftrain all its ftrings,
To pull me to 'em, from my ftern Refolve.
Husband, and Father ! All the melting Art
Of Eloquence lives in thofe foftning Names.
Methinks I fee the Babe, with Infant Hands,
Pleading for Life, and begging to be born;
Shall I forbid his Birth ? Deny him Light ?
The Heavenly Comforts of all cheering Light?
And make the Womb the Dungeon of his Death ?
His Bleeding Mother his fad Monument?
Thefe are the Calls of Nature, that call loud,
They will be heard, and Conquer in their Caufe;
He muft not be a Man, who can refift 'em.
No, my *Imoinda* ! I will venture all
To fave thee, and that little Innocent.
The World may be a better Friend to him,
Than I have found it.   Now I yield my felf.   [*Gives up his Sword.*
The Conflict's paft, and we are in your Hands.

    {*Several Men get about* Oroonoko, *and* Aboan, *and feize 'em.*
    Gov. So you fhall find you are ; Difpofe of them,
As I commanded you.

    Blan. Good Heaven forbid ! You cannot mean——
    Gov. This is not your Concern.   [*To* Blanford *who goes to* Oroonoko.
I muft take care of you.   [*To* Imoinda.

    Imo. I'm at the end
Of all my Care: Here I will die with him.   [*Holding* Oroonoko.
    Oro. You fhall not force her from me.   [*he holds her.*
    Gov. Then I muft   [*they force her from him.*
Try other means, and Conquer Force by Force :
Break, cut off his Held, bring her away.

    Imo. I do not ask to Live, kill me but here.

Or.

Oro. O bloody Dogs! inhuman Murderers.

Imoinda fore'd out of one Door by the Governor, and others.
Oroonoko and Aboan hurried out of another. Ex. Omnes.

ACT V. SCENE I.

Enter Stanmore, Lucia, Charlott.

Stan. 'TIS strange we cannot hear of him: Can no body give an account of him?

Luc. Nay, I begin to despair: I give him for gone.

Stan. Not so, I hope.

Luc. There are so many disturbances in this devilish Country! Wou'd we had never seen it.

Stan. This is but a cold welcome for you, Madam, after so troublesome a Voyage.

Char. A cold Welcome indeed, Sir, without my Cousin *Welldon*; he was the best Friend I had in the World.

Stan. He was a very good Friend of yours indeed, Madam.

Luc. They have made him away, murder'd him for his Money, I believe; he took a considerable Sum out with him, I know, that has been his Ruin.

Stan. That has done him no injury, to my knowledge: For this Morning he put into my Custody what you speak of, I suppose a Thousand Pounds, for the use of this Lady.

Char. I was always oblig'd to him; and he has shown his Care of me, in placing my little Affairs in such Honourable Hands.

Stan. He gave me a particular charge of you, Madam, very particular; so particular, that you will be surpriz'd when I tell you.

Char. What, pray Sir.

Stan. I am engag'd to get you a Husband, I promis'd that before I saw you; and now I have seen you, you must give me leave to offer you my self.

Luc. Nay, Cousin, never be coy upon the matter; to my knowledge my brother always design'd you for this Gentleman.

Stan. You hear, Madam, he has given me his Interest, and 'tis the Favour I wou'd have begg'd of him. Lord! you are so like him——

Char. That you are oblig'd to say you like me for his sake.

Stan. I shou'd be glad to love you for your own.

Char. If I shou'd consent to the fine things you can say to me, how wou'd you look at last, to find 'em thrown away upon an old Acquaintance?

Stan. An old Acquaintance!

Char. Lord, how easily are you Men to be impos'd upon! I am no Cousin newly arriv'd from *England*, not I; but the very *Welldon* you wot of.

Stan. *Welldon!*

Char. Not murder'd, nor made away, as my Sister wou'd have you believe, but am in very good Health, your old Friend in Breeches that was, and now your humble Servant in Petticoats.

Stan. I'm glad we have you agen.

But what service can you do me in Petticoats, pray?   *Char.*

G

Char. Can't you tell what?

Stan. Not I, by my troth: I have found my Friend, and loft my Miſtreſs, it ſeems, which I did not expeſt from your Petticoats.

Char. Come, come, you have had a Friend of your Miſtreſs long enough, 'tis high time now to have a Miſtreſs of your Friend.

Stan. What do you ſay?

Char. I am a Woman, Sir.

Stan. A Woman!

Char. As arrant a Woman as you wou'd have had me. But now, I aſſure you.

Stan. And at my Service?

Char. If you have any for me in Petticoats.

Stan. Yes, yes, I ſhall find you employment.

Char. You wonder at my proceeding, I believe.

Stan. 'Tis a little extraordinary, indeed.

Char. I have taken ſome pains to come into your Favour.

Stan. You might have had it cheaper a great deal.

Char. I might have marry'd you in the Perſon of my *Engliſh* Couſin, but cou'd not conſent to cheat you, ev'n in the thing I had a mind to.

Stan. 'Twas done as you do every thing.

Char. I need not tell you I made that little Plot, and carry'd it on only for this Opportunity. I was reſolv'd to ſee whether you lik'd me as a Woman, or not; if I had found you indifferent, I wou'd have endeavour'd to have been ſo too; but you ſay you like me, and therefore I have ventur'd to diſcover the truth.

Stan. Like you! I like you ſo well, that I'm afraid you won't think Marriage a proof on't: ſhall I give you any other?

Char. No, no, I'm inclin'd to believe you, and that ſhall convince me. At more leiſure I'll ſatisfy you how I came to be in Man's Cloaths, for no ill I aſſure you, tho' I have happen'd to play the Rogue in 'em. They have aſſiſted me in marrying my Siſter, and have gone a great way in befriending your Couſin *Jack* with the Widow. Can you forgive me for pimping for your Family?

Enter Jack Stanmore.

Stan. So, *Jack*, what News with you?

J. Stan. I am the forepart of the Widow, you know, She's coming after with the body of the Family, the young Squire in her hand, my Son-in Law that is to be, with the help of Mr. *Welldon.*

Char. Say you ſo, Sir?   [*Clapping* Jack *upon the back*

Enter Widow Lackitt with her Son Daniel.

Wid. So, Mrs. *Lucy*, I have brought him about agen, I have chaſtis'd him I have made him as ſupple as a Glove for your wearing, to pull on, or throw off, at your pleaſure. Will you ever Rebel again? Will you, Sirrah? But come, come, down on your Marrow-Bones, and aſk her forgiveneſs. [Daniel Kneels *Say after me; Pray forſooth Wife.*

Dan. Pray forſooth Wife.

Luc. Well, well, this is a Day of Good Nature, and ſo I take you into Favour. But firſt take the Oath of Allegiance. [*He kiſſes her Hand, and riſes* If ever you do ſo agen ——   D

Dan. Nay marry if I do, I shall have the worst on't.

Luc. Here's a Stranger, forsooth, wou'd be glad to be known to you, a Sister of mine, pray salute her.   [*starts at* Charlott.

Wid. Your Sister! Mrs. *Lucy!* what do you mean ? This is your Brother Mr. *Welldon*; do you think I do not know Mr. *Welldon* ?

Luc. Have a care what you say. This Gentleman's about Marrying her; You may spoil all.

Wid. Fiddle faddle, what! You wou'd put a trick upon me.

Char. No faith, Widow, the Trick is over, it has taken sufficiently, and now I will teach you the Trick,

To prevent your being Cheated another time.

Wid. How! Cheated, Mr. *Welldon.*

Char. Why, ay, you will always take things by the wrong Handle, I see you will have me Mr. *Welldon*: I grant you, I was Mr. *Welldon* a little while to please you, or so. But Mr. *Stanmore* here has perswaded me into a Woman agen.

Wid. A Woman! Pray let me speak with you.   [*drawing her aside.*
You are not in earnest, I hope? A Woman!

Char. Really a Woman.

Wid. Gad's my Life! I could not be cheated in every thing, I know a Man from a Woman at these Years, or the Devil's in't.

Pray, did not you marry me?

Char. You wou'd have it so.

Wid. And did not I give you a Thousand Pounds this Morning ?

Char. Yes indeed, 'twas more than I deserv'd ; But you had your Penniworth for your Penny, I suppose;

You seem'd to be pleas'd with your Bargain.

Wid. A rare Bargain, I have made on't, truly. I have laid out my Money to fine purpose upon a Woman.

Char. You wou'd have a Husband, and I provided for you as well as I cou'd.

Wid. Yes, yes, you have provided for me.

Char. And you have paid me very well for't, I thank you.

Wid. 'Tis very well; I may be with Child too, for ought I know, and may go look for the Father.

Char. Nay, if you think so, 'tis time to look about you indeed. Ev'n make up the matter as well as you can, I advise you as a Friend, and let us live Neighbourly and Lovingly together.

Wid. I have nothing else for it, that I know now.

Char. For my part, Mrs. *Lackitt*, your Thousand Pounds will Engage me not to laugh at you. Then my Sister is Married to your Son, he is to have half your Estate, I know; and indeed they may live upon it, very comfortably to themselves, and very creditably to you.

Wid. Nay, I can blame no body but my self.

Char. You have enough for a Husband still,

And that you may bestow upon honest *Jack Stanmore.*

Wid. Is he the Man then?

Char. He is the Man you are oblig'd to.

J Sta...

J. Stan. Yes, Faith, Widow, I am the Man: I have done fairly by you, you find, you know what you have to trust to before-hand.

Wid. Well, well, I see you will have me, ev'n Marry me, and make an end of the business.

Stan. Why, that's well said, now we are all agreed, and all provided for.

[*A Servant Enters to Stanmore.*

Serv. Sir, Mr. *Blandford* desires you to come to him, and bring as many of your Friends as you can with you.

Stan. I come to him. You'l all go along with me.
Come, young Gentleman, Marriage is the fashion, you see, you must like it now.

Dan. If I don't, how shall I help my self?

Luc. Nay, you may hang your self in the Noose, if you please,
But you'll never get out on't with struggling.

Dan. Come then, let's ev'n jogg on in the old Road.
Cuckold, or worse, I must be now contented:
I'm not the first has marry'd, and repented.   [*Exeunt.*

SCENE II.

Enter Governor with Blandford, and Planters.

Blan. Have you no Reverence of future Fame?
No awe upon your actions, from the Tongues,
The censuring Tongues of Men, that will be free?
If you confess Humanity, believe
There is a God, or Devil, to reward
Our doings here, do not provoke your Fate.
The Hand of Heaven is arm'd against these Crimes,
With hotter Thunder-Bolts, prepar'd to shoot,
And Nail you to the Earth, a sad Example;
A Monument of Faithless Infamy.

Enter Stanmore, J. Stanmore, Charlott, Lucy, Widow, and Daniel.
So, *Stanmore,* you I know, the Women too
Will join with me: 'Tis *Oroonoko's* Cause,
A Lover's Cause, a wretched Woman's Cause,
That will become your Intercession.   [*To the Women.*

1 *Plan.* Never mind 'em, Governour; he ought to be made an Example for the good of the Plantation.

2 *Plan.* Ay, ay, 'twill frighten the Negroes from Attempting the like agen.

1 *Plan.* What, rise against their Lords and Masters!
At this rate no Man is safe from his own Slaves.

2 *Plan.* No, no more he is. Therefore, one and all, Governour, we declare for Hanging.

Om. Plan. Ay, ay, hang him, hang him.

Wid. What! Hang him! O! forbid it, Governour.

Char.
Luc. } We all Petition for him.

J. Stan. They are for a Holy-Day; Guilty or not,
'Tis for the Business, Hanging is their Sport.

Blan.

Blan. We are not sure so wretched, to have these,
The Rabble, judge for us ; the changing Croud ;
The Arbitrary Guard of Fortune's Power,
Who wait to catch the Sentence of her Frowns,
And hurry all to ruin she Condemns.

Stan. So far from farther Wrong, that 'tis a shame
He shou'd be where he is : Good Governour
Order his Liberty : He yielded up
Himself, his all, at your discretion.

Blan. Discretion ! no, he yielded on your word ;
And I am made the cautionary Pledge,
The Gage, and Hostage of your keeping it.
Remember, Sir, he yielded on your word ;
Your word ! which honest Men will think should be
The last resort of Truth, and trust on Earth :
There's no Appeal beyond it, but to Heaven ;
An Oath is a recognisance to Heaven,
Binding us over, in the Courts above,
To plead the Indictment of our Crimes;
That those who 'scape this World should suffer there.
But in the common Intercourse of Men,
(Where the dread Majesty is not Invok'd,
His Honour not immediately concern'd
Not made a Party in our Interests,)
Our Word is all to be rely'd upon.

Wid. Come, come, You'l be as good as your Word, we know.

Stan. He's out of all power of doing any harm now,
If he were dispos'd to it.

Char. But he is not dispos'd to it.

Blan. To keep him, where he is, will make him soon
Find out some desperate way to Liberty ;
He'll hang himself, or dash out his mad Brains.

Char. Pray try him by gentle Means ;
We'll all be Sureties for him.

Om. All, all.

Luc. We will all answer for him now.

Gov. Well, you will have it so, do what you please,
Just what you will with him, I give you leave.   [*Exit.*

Blan. We thank you, Sir ; this way, pray come with me.   [*Exeunt.*

The Scene drawn shews Oroonoko *upon his Back, his Legs and
Arms stretcht out, and chain'd to the Ground.*

Enter Blandford, Stanmore, &c.

Bland. O miserable Sight ! help every one,
Assist me all to free him from his Chains.

                          [*They help him up, and bring him forward. looking down.*
Most injur'd Prince ! how shall we clear our selves ?
We cannot hope you will vouchsafe to hear,

Ox

Or credit what we fay in the Defence,
And Caufe of our fufpected Innocence.

Stan. We are not guilty of your Injuries,
No way confenting to 'em; but abhor,
Abominate, and loath this Cruelty.

Blan. It is our Curfe, but make it not our Crime.
A heavy Curfe upon us, that we muft
Share any thing in common, ev'n the Light,
The Elements, and Seafons, with fuch Men,
Whofe Principles, like the fam'd Dragons Teeth,
Scatter'd, and fown, wou'd fhoot a Harveft up
Of fighting Mifchiefs, to confound themfelves,
And ruin all about 'em.

Stan. Profligates!
Whofe bold *Titanian* Impiety
Wou'd once agen pollute their Mother Earth,
Force her to teem with her old monftrous Brood
Of Gyants, and forget the Race of Men.

Blan. We are not fo: believe us innocent.
We come prepar'd with all our Services,
To offer a Redrefs of your bafe W rorg
Which way fhall we employ 'em?

Stan. Tell us, Sir, if there is any thing that can atone;
But nothing can; that may be fome amends———

Oro. If you wou'd have me think you are not all
Confederates, all acceffory to
The bafe Injuftice of your Governour;
If you wou'd have me live, as you appear
Concern'd for me, if you wou'd have me live
To thank, and blefs you, there is yet a Way
To tye me ever to your honeft Love;
Bring my *Imoinda* to me; give me her,
To charm my Sorrows, and, if poffible,
I'le fit down with my Wrongs; never to rife
Againft my Fate, or think of Vengeance more.

Blan. Be fatish'd, you may depend upon us,
We'll bring her fafe to you, and fuddenly.

Char. We wonnot leave you in fo good a work.

VVid. No, no, we'll go with you.

Blan. In the mean time
Endeavour to forget, Sir, and forgive;
And hope a better Fortune.

                              Oroonoko *alone.*

Oro. Forget! forgive! I muft indeed forget,
When I forgive; but while I am a Man,
In Flefh, that bears the living mark of Shame,
The print of his difhonourable Chains,
My Memory ftill rouling up my Wrongs,

I never can forgive this Governour;
This Villain; the difgrace of Truft, and Place,
And juft Contempt of delegated Power.
What fhall I do? If I declare my felf,
I know him, he will fneak behind his Guard
Of Followers, and brave me in his Fears.
Elfe, Lyon-like, with my devouring Rage,
I wou'd rufh on him, faften on his Throat,
Tear wide a Paffage to his treacherous Heart,
And that way lay him open to the World.   [*Paufing.*
If I fhou'd turn his Chriftian Arts on him,
Promife him, fpeak him fair, flatter, and creep,
With fawning Steps, to get within his Faith,
I cou'd betray him then, as he has me,
But am I fure by that to right my felf?
Lying's a certain Mark of Cowardife;
And when the Tongue forgets its Honefty,
The Heart and Hand may drop their functions too,
And nothing worthy be refolv'd, or done.
The Man muft go together, bad, or good;
In one part frail, he foon grows weak in all.
Honour fhou'd be concern'd in Honour's Caufe,
That is not to be cur'd by Contraries,
As Bodies are, whofe Health is often drawn
From rankeft Poyfons.   Let me but find out
An honeft Remedy, I have the Hand,
A miniftring Hand, that will apply it Home.   [*Exit.*

S C E N E *the Governor's Houfe.*

Enter Governor.

Gov. I wou'd not have her tell me fhe confents;
In Favour of the Sexes Modefty,
That ftill fhou'd be prefum'd, becaufe there is
A greater Impudence in owning it,
Than in allowing all that we can do.
This Truth I know, and yet againft my felf,
(So unaccountable are Lovers ways)
I talk, and lofe the Opportunities,
Which Love, and fhe expects I fhou'd employ :
Ev'n fhe expects : for when a Man has faid
All that is fit, to fave the Decency,
The Women know the reft is to be done.
I wonnot difappoint her.   [*Going.*

Enter to him Blanford, *the* Stanmores, Daniel, *Mrs.* Lackitt, Charlot,
and Lucy.

Wid. O Governor! I'm glad we have lit upon you.
Gov. Why! what's the matter?

Cha

(50)

Char. Nay, nothing extraordinary. But one good Action
Draws on another. You have given the Prince his Freedom :
Now we come a begging for his Wife :
You won't refuse us.

Gov. Refuse you. No, no, what have I to do to refuse you ?

Wid. You won't refuse to send her to him, she means.

Gov. I send her to him !

Wid. We have promis'd him to bring her.

Gov. You do very well ; 'tis kindly done of you.
Ev'n carry her to him, with all my heart.

Luc. You must tell us where she is.

Gov. I tell you ! why, don't you know ?

Blan. Your Servants say she's in the House.

Gov. No, no, I brought her home at first indeed ; but I thought it would
not look well to keep her here : I remov'd her in the Hurry, only to take
care of her. What ! she belongs to you : I have nothing to do with her.

Char. But where is she now, Sir ?

Gov. Why, Faith, I can't say certainly : you'll hear of her at *Parham*
House, I suppose : there, or thereabouts : I think I sent her there.

Blan. I'll have an Eye on him   [*Aside.*
                                              [*Exeunt all but the Governor.*

Gov. I have ly'd my self into a little Time ;
And must employ it : they'll be here agen ;
But I must be before 'em.   [*Going out, he meets* Imoinda, *and seizes her.*
Are you come !
I'll court no longer for a Happiness
That is in mine own keeping : you may still
Refuse to grant, so I have power to take.
The Man that asks, deserves to be deny'd.
          [*She disingages one hand, and draws his Sword from his side upon him.* Governor
                    starts and retires. Blanford *enters behind him.*

Imo. He does indeed, that asks unworthily.

Blan. You hear her, Sir, that asks unworthily.

Gov. You are no Judge.

Blan. I am of my own Slave.

Gov. Be gone and leave us.

Blan. When you let her go.

Gov. To fasten upon you.

Blan. I must defend my self.

Imo. Help, Murder, help.
          [Imoinda *retreats towards the door, favour'd by* Blanford, *when they are clos'd,*
                    she throws down the Sword, and runs out. Governor *takes up the Sword,*
                    they fight, close, and fall, Blanford *upon him. Servants enter, and part 'em.*

Gov. She shannot scape me so. I've gone too far,
Not to go farther. Curse on my delay :
But yet she is, and shall be in my Power.

Blan. Nay, then it is the War of Honesty :
I know you, and will save you from your self.

Gov. All come along with me.   [*Exeunt.*

                                                            SCENE

SCENE *the laſt*

Oroonoko *enters.*

Oro. To Honour bound! and yet a Slave to Love!
I am diſtracted by their rival Powers,
And both will be obey'd.   O great Revenge!
Thou Raiſer, and Reſtorer of faln Fame!
Let me not be unworthy of thy Aid,
For ſtopping in thy courſe: I ſtill am thine:
But can't forget I am *Imoinda*'s too.
She calls me from my Wrongs to reſcue her.
No man condemns me, who has ever felt
A Woman's Power, or try'd the Force of Love:
All tempers yield, and ſoften in thoſe fires:
Our Honours, Intereſts reſolving down,
Run in the gentle Current of our Joys;
But not to ſink, and drown our Memory;
We mount agen to Action, like the Sun,
That riſes from the Boſom of the Sea,
To run his glorious Race of Light anew,
And carry on the World.   Love, Love will be
My firſt Ambition, and my Fame the next.

Aboan *enters bloody.*

My Eyes are turn'd againſt me, and combine
With my ſworn Enemies, to repreſent
This Spectacle of Honour.   *Aboan*!
My ever faithful Friend!

Abo. I have no Name,
That can diſtinguiſh me from the vile Earth,
To which I'm going; a poor abject Worm,
That crawl'd a-while upon a buſtling World,
And now am trampled to my Duſt agen.

Oro. I ſee thee gaſht and mangled.

Abo. Spare my ſhame
To tell how they have us'd me; but believe
The Hangman's Hand wou'd have been merciful.
Do not you ſcorn me, Sir, to think I can
Intend to live under this Infamy.
I do not come for pity, to complain.
I've ſpent an honourable Life with you;
The earlieſt Servant of your riſing Fame,
And wou'd attend it with my lateſt care;
My Life was yours, and ſo ſhall be my Death.
You muſt not live.
Bending and ſinking, I have dragg'd my ſteps
Thus far, to tell you that you cannot live:
To warn you of thoſe Ignominious wrongs,

H

Whips, Rods, and all the Inſtruments of death,
Which I have felt, and are prepar'd for you.
This was the Duty that I had to pay.
'Tis done, and now I beg to be diſcharg'd.

   Oro. What ſhall I do for thee?

   Abo. My Body tires,
And wonnot bear me off to Liberty;
I ſhall agen be taken, made a Slave.
A Sword, a Dagger yet wou'd reſcue me.
I have not Strength to go to find out Death;
You muſt direct him to me.

   Oro. Here he is,   [*Gives him a Dagger.*
The only preſent I can make thee now;
And next the honourable means of Life,
I wou'd beſtow the honeſt means of Death.

   Abo. I cannot ſtay to thank you. If there is
A Being after this, I ſhall be yours
In the next World, your faithful Slave agen.
This is to try [*Stabs himſelf.*] I had a living Senſe,
Of all your royal Favours, but this laſt
Strikes through my Heart. I wonnot ſay farewell,
For you muſt follow me.   [*dies.*

   Oro. In Life, and Death,
The Guardian of my Honour! follow thee!
I ſhou'd have gone before thee; then perhaps
Thy Fate had been prevented. All his Care
Was to preſerve me from the barbarous Rage
That wrong'd him, only for being mine.
Why, why, you Gods! Why am I ſo accurſt,
That it muſt be a Reaſon of your Wrath,
A Guilt, a Crime ſufficient to the Fate
Of any one, but to belong to me?
My Friend has found it, and my Wife will ſoon;
My Wife! the very Fear's too much for Life;
I can't ſupport it. Where? *Imoinda!* Oh!
              [*Going out, ſhe meets him, running into his Arms.*
Thou boſom Softneſs! Down of all my Cares!
I cou'd recline my thoughts upon this Breaſt
To a forgetfulneſs of all my Griefs,
And yet be happy; but it wonnot be.
Thou art diſorder'd, pale, and out of Breath!
If Fate purſues thee, find a ſhelter here.
What is it thou wou'dſt tell me?

   Imo. 'Tis in vain to call him Villain.

   Oro. Call him Governour; is it not ſo?

   Imo. There's not another ſure.

   Oro. Villain's the common name of Mankind here;
But his moſt properly. What! what of him?

I fear to be refolv'd, and muft enquire.
He had thee in his Power.

   Imo. I blufh to think it.

   Oro. Blufh! to think what?

   Imo. That I was in his Power.

   Oro. He cou'd not ufe it ?

   Imo. What can't fuch men do ?

   Oro. But did he ? durft he ?

   Imo. What he cou'd, he dar'd.

   Oro. His own Gods damn him then ; for ours have none,
No Punifhment for fuch unheard-of Crimes.

   Imo. This Monfter, cunning in his Flatteries,
When he had weary'd all his ufclefs Arts,
Leapt out, fierce as a beaft of prey, to feize me.
I trembled, fear'd.

   Oro. I fear, and tremble now.
What cou'd preferve thee? what deliver thee ?

   Imo. That worthy Man, you us'd to call your Friend---

   Oro. Blanford.

   Imo. Came in, and fav'd me from his Rage.

   Oro. He was a Friend indeed to refcue thee !
And for his fake I'll think it poffible
A Chriftian may be yet an honeft man.

   Imo. O! did you know what I have ftrugl'd through
To fave me yours, fure you wou'd promife me
Never to fee me forc't from you agen.

   Oro. To promife thee ! O ! do I need to promife ?
But there is now no farther ufe of Words.
Death is fecurity for all our fears.   [*Shews* Aboan's *Body on the floor.*
And yet I cannot truft him.

   Imo. Aboan !

   Oro. Mangled, and torn, refolv'd to give me time
To fit my felf for what I muft expect,
Groan'd out a warning to me, and expir'd.

   Imo. For what you muft expect ?

   Oro. Wou'd that were all.

   Imo. What ! to be butcher'd thus ———

   Oro. Juft as thou fee'lt.

   Imo. By barbarous Hands, to fall at laft their Prey!

   Oro. I have run the Race with Honour, fhall I now
Lag, and be overtaken at the Goal ?

   Imo. No.

   Oro. I muft look back to thee.   *Tenderly.*

   Imo. You fhannot need.
I'm always prefent to your purpofe, fay,
Which way wou'd you difpofe me ?

   Oro. Have a care,
Thou'rt on a Precipice, and doft not fee

Whither that Queſtion leads thee. O ! too ſoon
Thou doſt enquire what the aſſembled Gods
Have not determin'd, and will lateſt doom.
Yet this I know of Fate, this is moſt certain,
I cannot, as I wou'd, diſpoſe of thee :
And, as I ought, I dare not. Oh *Imoinda !*

Imo. Alas ! that ſigh ! why do you tremble ſo ?
Nay then 'tis bad indeed, if you can weep.

Oro. My Heart runs over ; if my guſhing Eyes
Betray a weakneſs which they never knew,
Believe, thou, only thou cou'dſt cauſe theſe tears.
The Gods themſelves conſpire with faithleſs Men
To our deſtruction.

Imo. Heaven and Earth our Foes !

Oro. It is not always granted to the great,
To be moſt happy : If the angry Pow'rs
Repent their Favours, let 'em take 'em back ;
The hopes of Empire, which they gave my youth,
By making me a Prince, I here reſign.
Let 'em quench in me all thoſe glorious Fires,
Which kindled at their Beams ; that luſt of Fame,
That Fever of Ambition, reſtleſs ſtill,
And burning with the ſacred Thirſt of Sway,
Which they inſpir'd, to qualify my Fate,
And make me fit to govern under them,
Let 'em extinguiſh. I ſubmit my ſelf
To their high pleaſure, and devoted Bow
Yet lower, to continue ſtill a Slave ;
Hopeleſs of Liberty ; and if I cou'd
Live after it, wou'd give up Honour too,
To ſatisfy their Vengeance, to avert
This only Curſe, the Curſe of loſing thee.

Imo. If Heav'n cou'd be appeas'd, theſe cruel Men
Are not to be entreated, or believ'd ;
O ! think on that, and be no more deceiv'd.

Oro. What can we do ?

Imo. Can I do any thing ?

Oro. But we were born to ſuffer.

Imo. Suffer both,
Both die, and ſo prevent 'em.

Oro. By thy Death !
O ! Let me hunt my Travell'd Thoughts again ;
Range the wide waſte of deſolate deſpair ;
Start any hope. Alas ! I loſe my ſelf,
'Tis Pathleſs, Dark, and Barren all to me.
Thou art my only Guide, my light of Life,
And thou art leaving me ; Send out thy Beams
Upon the Wing ; let 'em fly all around,

Diſcover every way ; Is there a dawn,
A glimmering of comfort? the great God,
That riſes on the world, muſt ſhine on us.

Imo. And ſee us ſet before him.

Oro. Thou beſpeak'ſt, and goes before me.

Imo. So I wou'd in Love ;
In the dear unſuſpected part of Life,
In Death for Love. Alas ! what hopes for me ?
I was preſerv'd but to acquit my ſelf,
To beg to die with you.

Oro. And can'ſt thou ask it ?
I never durſt enquire into my ſelf
About thy fate, and thou reſolv'ſt it all.

Imo. Alas! my Lord ! my Fate's reſolv'd in yours.

Oro. O ! keep thee there: Let not thy Virtue ſhrink
From my ſupport, and I will gather ſtrength,
Faſt as I can to tell thee ————

Imo. I muſt die.
I know 'tis fit, and I can die with you.

Oro. O ! thou haſt baniſht hence a thouſand fears,
Which ſickned at my Heart, and quite unman'd me.

Imo. Your fear's for me, I know you fear'd my ſtrength,
And cou'd not overcome your tenderneſs,
To paſs this Sentence on me: and indeed
There you were kind, as I have always found you,
As you have ever been : for tho' I am
Reſign'd, and ready to obey my doom,
Methinks it ſhou'd not be pronounc'd by you.

Oro. O ! that was all the labour of my grief.
My heart, and tongue forſook me in the ſtrife :
I never cou'd pronounce it.

Imo. I have for you, for both of us.

Oro. Alas ! for me ! my death
I cou'd regard as the laſt Scene of life,
And act it through with joy, to have it done.
But then to part with thee ————

Imo. 'Tis hard to part.
But parting thus, as the moſt happy muſt,
Parting in death, makes it the eaſier.
You might have thrown me off, forſaken me,
And my misfortunes: that had been a death
Indeed of terror, to have trembled at.

Oro. Forſaken, thrown thee off!

Imo. But 'tis a pleaſure more than life can give,
That with unconquer'd Paſſion to the laſt,
You ſtruggle ſtill, and fain wou'd hold me to you.

Oro. Ever, ever, and let thoſe ſtars, which are my Enemies,
Witneſs againſt me in the other World,

If I wou'd leave this Manfion of my Blifs,
To be the brighteft Ruler of their Skies.
O! that we cou'd incorporate, be one,   [Embracing her.
One Body, as we have been long one Mind;
That blended fo, we might together mix,
And lofing thus our Beings to the World,
Be only found to one another's Joys.
   Imo. Is this the way to part?
   Oro. Which is the way?
   Imo. The God of Love is blind, and cannot find it.
But quick, make hafte, our Enemies have Eyes
To find us out, and fhew us the worft way
Of parting; think on them.
   Oro. Why doft thou wake me?
   Imo. O! no more of Love,
For if I liften to you, I fhall quite
Forget my Dangers, and defire to live.
I can't live yours.   [Takes up the Dagger.
   Oro. There all the Stings of Death
Are fhot into my Heart —— what fhall I do?
   Imo. This Dagger will inftruct you.   [Gives it him.
   Oro. Ha! this Dagger!
Like Fate, it points me to the horrid Deed.
   Imo. Strike, ftrike it home, and bravely fave us both.
There is no other Safety.
   Oro. It muft be——
But firft a dying Kifs——   [Kiffes her.
This laft Embrace ——   [Embracing her.
And now——
   Imo. I'm ready.
   Oro. O! where fhall I ftrike?
Is there a fmalleft grain of that lov'd Body
That is not dearer to me than my Eyes,
My bofom'd Heart, and all the live Blood there?
Bid me cut off thefe Limbs, hew off thefe Hands,
Dig out thefe Eyes, tho' I wou'd keep them laft
To gaze upon thee. But to murder thee!
The Joy, and Charm of every ravifht Senfe,
My Wife! forbid it Nature.
   Imo. 'Tis your Wife,
Who on her knees conjures you. O! in time
Prevent thofe Mifchiefs that are falling on us.
You may be hurry'd to a fhameful Death,
And I too drag'd to the vile Governeur;
Then I may cry aloud; when you are gone,
Where fhall I find a Friend agen to fave me?
   Oro. It will be fo. Thou unexampled Virtue!
Thy Refolution has recover'd mine:
And now prepare thee.   *Im*

Imo. Thus with open Arms,
I welcome you, and Death.

    [*He drops his Dagger as he looks on her, and throws himself on the Ground.*

Oro. I cannot bear it.
O let me dash against this Rock of Fate.
Dig up this Earth, tear, tear her Bowels out,
To make a Grave, deep as the Center down,
To swallow wide, and bury us together.
It wonnot be. O! then some pitying God
(If there be one a Friend to Innocence)
Find yet a way to lay her Beauties down
Gently in Death, and save me from her Blood.

Imo. O rise, 'tis more than Death to see you thus,
I'le ease your Love, and do the Deed my self——

    [*She takes up the Dagger, he rises in haste to take it from her.*

Oro. O! hold, I charge thee, hold.

Imo. Tho' I must own
It wou'd be nobler for us both from you.

Oro. O! for a Whirlwind's Wing to hurry us
To yonder Cliff, which frowns upon the Flood;
That in Embraces lockt we might plunge in,
And perish thus in one anothers Arms.

Imo. Alas! what shout is that?

Oro. I see 'em coming.
They shannot overtake us. This last Kiss,
And now farwell.

Imo. Farewel, farewel for ever.

Oro. I'le turn my Face away, and do it so.
Now, are you ready?

Imo. Now. But do not grudge me
The Pleasure in my Death of a last look,
Pray look upon me——Now I'm satisfied.

Oro. So Fate must be by this

    [*Going to stab her, he stops short, she lays her hands on his, in order to give the blow.*

Imo. Nay then I must assist you.
And since it is the common Cause of both,
'Tis just that both shou'd be employ'd in it.
Thus, thus 'tis finisht, and I bless my Fate,   [*Stabs her self.*
That where I liv'd, I die, in these lov'd Arms.   [*Dyes.*

Oro. She's gone. And now all's at an End with me.
Soft, lay her down. O we will part no more.   [*Throws himself by her.*
But let me pay the tribute of my Grief,
A few sad Tears to thy lov'd Memory,
And then I follow ——   [*Weeps over her.*
But I stay too long.   [*A noise agen.*
The Noise comes nearer. Hold, before I go,

There's

There's something wou'd be done.   It ſhall be ſo.
And then, *Imoinda,* I'le come all to thee.   [*Riſes.*
          [*Blanford and his party, enters before the Governor and his
                    party, Swords drawn on both ſides.*
    Gov. You ſtrive in vain to ſave him, he ſhall die.
    Blan. Not while we can defend him with our lives.
    Gov Where is he?
    Oro. Here's the Wretch whom you wou'd have.
Put up your Swords, and let not civil broils
Engage you in the curſed cauſe of one,
Who cannot live, and now entreats to die.
This object will convince you.
    Blan. 'Tis his Wife!   [*They gather about the Body*
Alas! there was no other Remedy.
    Gov. Who did the bloody Deed?
    Oro. The Deed was mine;
Bloody I know it is, and I expect
Your Laws ſhou'd tell me ſo.   Thus ſelf-condemn'd,
I do reſign my ſelf into your Hands,
The Hands of Juſtice———But I hold the Sword
For you—and for my ſelf.
          [*Stabs the Governour, and himſelf, then throws himſelf by* Imoinda's *Body.*
    Stan. He has kill'd the Governor, and ſtab'd himſelf.
    Oro. 'Tis as it ſhou'd be now.   I have ſent his Ghoſt
To be a Witneſs of that Happineſs
In the next World, which he deny'd us here.   [*Dyes.*
    Blan. I hope there is a place of Happineſs
In the next World for ſuch exalted Virtue.
Pagan, or Unbeliever, yet he liv'd
To all he knew; And if he went aſtray,
There's Mercy ſtill above to ſet him right.
But Chriſtians guided by the Heavenly Ray,
Have no excuſe if we miſtake our Way.

F I N I S.